SA.

IN HI, COMMUNITY

Saint Benedict
in his Community

Richard Newman

Gracewing

First published in England in 2022
by
Gracewing
2 Southern Avenue
Leominster
Herefordshire HR6 0QF
United Kingdom
www.gracewing.co.uk

All rights reserved

No part of this publication may be reproduced, stored in a retrieval system, or transmitted in any form or by any means, electronic, mechanical, photocopying, recording or otherwise, without the written permission of the publisher.

© 2022, Richard Newman

The right of Richard Newman to be identified as the author of this work has been asserted in accordance with the Copyright, Designs and Patents Act 1988.

ISBN 978 085244 989 9

Cover design by Bernardita Peña Hurtado
Typeset by Word and Page, Chester, UK

Contents

PREFACE	vii
1. Saint Benedict in his Times	1
2. Roman Italy under Gothic Rule	5
3. Religious Life under Gothic Rule	21
4. Benedict as a Student	33
5. Benedict Leaves Rome	55
6. The Church Divided	59
7. The Monastery in the World	81
8. The Community at Home	113
9. Ways of Prayer	137
EXCURSUSES	161
NOTES	209
INDEX	229

Preface

After I retired from my work as a university lecturer, my wife and I moved to the south of England, where we found ourselves only a short distance from the Benedictine community that was then at Elmore Abbey, on the outskirts of Newbury. We eventually became oblates of the community and spent many days with the monks, sharing their life of prayer and work, their psalmody and their silence. I began to study Saint Benedict's *Rule for Monks* and the hagiographical *Life of Saint Benedict* by Gregory the Great—the second of his *Dialogues*—as well as commentaries on both of these works. As a historian, I naturally began to ask questions about the society in which Saint Benedict lived. None of the commentaries was able to satisfy my curiosity, so I decided to do some research of my own. At first I had no intention of writing anything on the subject; then I thought a pamphlet might be sufficient, but that expanded into a small volume which was published in 2013. Now, after much revision and extension, that volume has become the present book.

There is much to admire in the existing commentaries on the *Rule* and the *Dialogue* because of their scholarship and the many insights which they offer into Benedict's spirituality. There are, nevertheless, advantages in adding a historical perspective; it helps us to understand the challenges which

Benedict faced and increases our appreciation of his achievement. The historical context also helps us to understand some aspects of the original texts which I believe have been misunderstood, or not given sufficient weight.

Saint Benedict belonged to two communities: the community of monks which he formed and led, and the wider community of late Roman Italy, in which he and his monks were brought up and lived out their lives. It is the relationship between these two communities that is examined in this book.

My first book, *Saint Benedict in his Time*, was published by Three Peaks Press in 2013. I am very grateful to the publisher, Michael Woodward, for seeing my manuscript into print and for helping me to refine my ideas. Most of my research was done in the Bodleian Library at Oxford and I am much indebted to the librarian and staff for allowing me access to their excellent collections. I am also indebted to the staff of the library at Hereford Cathedral.

My interest in monasticism has been encouraged by a number of fine teachers and role models. I first became acquainted with the subject at a lovely retreat house in Wales, run by Mary Lewis, with Victor de Waal as retreat leader and Esther de Waal as a speaker. When my wife and I went to live near Newbury we found ourselves close not only to Elmore but also to Douai Abbey and I went to a number of retreats there and benefited greatly from talking to members of the community. I am now fortunate to be living near Hereford, with the monks of Belmont

Abbey as neighbours. My greatest debt, however, is to the late Dom Basil Matthews and the monks of Elmore Abbey, now removed to St Benedict's Priory in Salisbury. They offered me much hospitality and showed me how Benedict's *Rule* might become the foundation of everyday life.

Above all, my thanks go to my wife, Sheila, for her perceptive comments on the *Rule* and her loving support throughout my years of study and writing.

Richard Newman,
Hereford
May 2022

1

Saint Benedict in his Times

THE FEW DETAILS we have about the life of Saint Benedict sit lightly on the history of his times. This is partly because so little is known for certain about Benedict himself. It is generally believed that he was born about 480 CE, the son of a prosperous family in Nursia (Norcia) in the Italian region of Umbria. After a short period of education in Rome, followed by experiences as a hermit and then—briefly—as the abbot of an unruly community of monks at Vicovaro, he successfully founded a cluster of small monasteries at Subiaco, near Rome. About 529, he took some of his monks to Monte Cassino, a prominent hill overlooking the road from Rome to Naples. There they constructed a new monastery and it was there that Benedict wrote a rule for his monks and lived until his death, probably in about 547.

Most of what we know about Benedict comes from the second *Dialogue* of Pope Gregory the Great (abbreviated hereafter as *Dialogue*), which is filled with stories of miracles and prophecies, but has very few of the facts that we would normally expect in a biography.[1] Gregory's account has been analysed by many commentators and there is general agreement that its main purpose is to inspire the reader with the example of Benedict's holiness. Indeed, some commentators have suggested that few of the details should be taken literally or regarded as historically accurate.[2] Nevertheless, there are incidents in the *Dialogue* that can be related to actual events, even if Gregory has put his own particular gloss on them, and the rest of the book is not inconsistent with what is known about the Italy of Benedict's day.

In recent times, professional historians have given us a picture of Italian life in the fifth and sixth centuries in ever-increasing detail, a picture of social and political upheaval and of a Church that was struggling to resolve theological conflicts and establish a centralised administration. Very little of this contextual material has found its way into the commentaries either on the *Dialogue* or on Benedict's own *Rule* for monks, the *Regula Benedicti* (abbreviated as *RB*).[3] It is true that Benedict was writing a rule of life for an enclosed community with spiritual goals and one would not expect him to comment on the world outside, yet there are oblique references to that world and it is hard to believe that Benedict was not affected by it. This is not to deny the importance of the Bible and Church traditions in shaping Benedict's ideas; rather, it is to try to recognise how far Benedict was working with the grain of contemporary beliefs and customs and how far he was cutting across them. In this way we can appreciate more fully his achievement in building a monastic community that was successful in its own times and in writing a *Rule* that has been timeless in its appeal.

2

Roman Italy under Gothic Rule

BENEDICT'S LIFE coincides almost exactly with the rule of Ostrogothic kings over the Italian peninsula. The Roman emperors had long since moved their capital to Constantinople, leaving a western emperor as viceroy, based either in Rome or in the northern capital of Ravenna. In 476 there was a mutiny in the Roman army in Italy over the soldiers' pay and conditions. In fact, the army was Roman in name only; during the previous century, more and more of its units had been recruited from tribal people, from Goths and other ethnic groups who lived on the frontiers of the empire. The mutineers chose a Gothic general, Odoacar, as their leader and proclaimed him king. Odoacar bundled the western emperor into retirement and sent his imperial regalia back to Constantinople, along with a message, endorsed by the Roman senate, saying that it was quite sufficient for Italy to share a single emperor with the rest of the empire. Odoacar also made it clear that in matters relating to Italy, he alone was in charge.

Meanwhile, the emperor in Constantinople was having Gothic problems nearer home.[1] There were several groups of Ostrogoths (eastern Goths) in central and eastern Europe, particularly those of Pannonia (southern Hungary), led by the Amal clan, and those of Thrace (Bulgaria), who were only a short march from the imperial capital. The situation became more threatening when the young Amal chieftain, Theoderic, led his people southwards in a direct challenge to both the emperor and the Thracian Ostrogoths. The aim of these tribes was to make such a nuisance of themselves—disturbing the countryside and backing dissident factions at court—that the emperor would buy them off with subsidies of gold. At the same time the tribes did their best to eliminate each other as competitors. Theoderic played this dangerous game with considerable success until the emperor managed to divert his attention towards Italy where, it was suggested, he might replace Odoacar as the local overlord. The years 489–93 saw Theoderic campaigning in northern Italy, but Odoacar was not easy to dislodge and eventually the two leaders agreed to rule Italy jointly. Less than a fortnight after this agreement came into force, at a banquet in the royal palace in Ravenna, Theoderic suddenly drew his sword and with a single blow almost cut Odoacar in half. Theoderic thus became king of Italy.[2]

After this violent overture, the rest of Theoderic's long reign was remarkably tranquil. The ending of hostilities allowed trade to move freely and food prices to fall. The government was able to collect taxes more smoothly and to embark on public building projects such as aqueducts, amphitheatres and land reclamation schemes. The old elites continued to guide the affairs of their towns and cities. The first half of Benedict's adult life was therefore a time of stability and peace.

One of Theoderic's earliest problems was getting his followers to settle on Italian soil. This was gradually accomplished by finding them land and granting them a share of local taxes, a task that required many delicate negotiations with existing landowners. Most of the Goths were settled in an arc across the north of the country from Liguria (Lombardy) to Venetia and along the northern half of the Adriatic coast in places where they would block the main invasion routes from Gaul and Dalmatia and protect the northern plains from seaborne attack. There was a sizeable community of Goths in Rome and there were also scattered garrisons further south. The Goths kept a sense of Gothic identity, distinct from that of the Italo-Roman majority, through their military role in Italian society, through the special administrative arrangements which Theoderic made for them and through their attachment to the unorthodox beliefs of Arian Christianity.

The size of the Gothic minority is far from clear. The consensus among historians is that Theoderic came to Italy with an army of about 20,000, increased to a total of about 100,000 by wives and families, which was then augmented a little by stragglers from Thrace and the remnants of Odoacar's forces.[3] What is certain, however, is that Italy was not swamped by Gothic hordes, as some writers used to claim. Indeed, in some parts of the country—and especially in the south—people probably went about their daily business without ever meeting a Goth.

Theoderic was always anxious to assert his legitimacy as ruler of Italy. To remove any doubts on this score he tried to be as Roman as possible in his lifestyle and his policies. His palace in Ravenna followed the design of a very grand Roman villa, with a bronze equestrian statue of himself at the entrance, and his chapel was decorated with mosaics suggesting that he too, like the Roman emperor, was a viceroy of God upon earth. When Theoderic visited Rome in 500 he entered the city in triumph, like the emperors of old: he met the senate in the Forum, mounted circus games for the city's population, distributed grain to the poor and set up a fund for the repair of ancient monuments. In fact, this was Theoderic's only visit to Rome; during the rest of his reign he wisely decided not to get too involved in the city's politics and left it to local leaders to sort out their problems. However, he was respectful towards the senate and took notice of its opinions, he nominated leading members of it to important offices of state and he recruited members of aristocratic families to join him in Ravenna and run his administration.

This policy of *romanitas* (or Roman-ness) became one of the guiding principles of public life. Theoderic promoted classical education and set an example by educating members of his own family; the classics, he claimed, taught rationality and self-control and therefore helped to create a moral society. He used the existing Roman tax system. He maintained the code of Roman law, adding to it, where necessary, with edicts of his own but avoiding a wholesale reform. These policies upheld the values and social position of the wealthy landowning class who dominated the politics of the senate and ran the towns and country districts all over Italy.

It is very likely that Benedict came from this class. His father probably had a modest estate in the countryside near Nursia and a substantial house inside the town. He would have spent his time talking to other prominent citizens about the local tax burden, the town's food supply, the wearisome business of repairing the town wall—Theoderic was very insistent on the upkeep of town walls—and the maintenance of public order generally.[4] If the young Benedict had overheard his father doing business, as he probably did, he would have had a good understanding of the problems of governing a small urban community.

Theoderic's policies were the ingredients of *civilitas*, the Roman ideal of a society living under a written law. Of course, things did not always work out as Theoderic intended. There was a certain amount of friction between communities, especially when the law was warped by corruption. Goths were still rather inclined to rough-up their Italo-Roman neighbours; having been raised for a life of plunder and excitement, Gothic warriors found it difficult to settle down on their allotments on the outskirts of

Saint Benedict in his Community

Ravenna or Verona. Nevertheless, Theoderic's Italy was remarkably stable and orderly. Benedict therefore grew up in a country that was not only peaceful but was essentially Roman, the final flowering of Roman society in Italy. 'St Benedict', says the historian of monasticism, Dom David Knowles, 'is one of the last of the Romans ... [giving] the impression of sanity, of strength, of moderation and of stability — typical qualities of the noblest Romans.'[5]

This state of affairs was about to change as Italy was about to enter a period of conflict and confusion. Theoderic's careful statecraft was undone by the fact that he had no son and the succession ran through his daughter Amalasuntha to his grandson Athalaric. When Theoderic died in 526 Athalaric was only about ten and ruled under the regency of his mother. Amalasuntha was determined and politically astute, but the Gothic military elite was reluctant to take orders from a woman and a callow youth. The situation worsened in 534 when Athalaric died prematurely and the Gothic court dissolved into factions.[6] The Roman emperor Justinian,[7] watching these developments from his eastern capital, decided that this was an opportune moment to intervene and bring Italy under his direct rule.

In 535 Justinian sent an army westwards from Constantinople under his foremost general, Belisarius.[8] After securing Sicily, the emperor's Byzantine forces crossed in 536 to the mainland and fought their way from Naples to the north, finally capturing Ravenna.[9] In 540 the Goths were persuaded to surrender in the belief that they would keep some degree of autonomy, but this proved to be illusory; instead, they found themselves controlled by corrupt Byzantine bureaucrats, led by a man known as 'Snips' because he made profitable use of a device that snipped the edge off gold coins without spoiling their circular appearance. He and his subordinates took a cut from much else besides. The Goths rose in revolt and in 541 they mustered a new army, elected a new leader, Totila, and battled their way back to the south.

Over the next few years Totila was able to re-take the major cities, including Rome and Naples, raid Sicily, build a navy and keep Belisarius on the defensive, but in 552 a fresh Byzantine army under a new commander invaded Italy from the north-east, straight into the Gothic heartlands, so that Ravenna was quickly captured, the Goths defeated, and Totila killed. Some small detachments of Goths survived and were mopped up over the next decade. However, Justinian's success was short-lived. During the next fifty years, successive waves of Lombard and Frankish invaders poured into Italy and the country settled into a pattern of political division and intermittent warfare which lasted many centuries. The last twenty years of Benedict's life—his years at Monte Cassino—were therefore a time of war, misery and upheaval, the final destruction of the Roman social and political order.

Looking down from their monastery windows, the monks would have been reminded of the war

Saint Benedict in his Community

by the sight of armies passing up and down the Via Latina followed by their ox-drawn supply wagons, hundreds of them in processions that stretched for miles and took hours to pass. One of these processions must have been the backdrop to Totila's visit to Benedict at Monte Cassino (*Dialogue* 14.1–15.2), which probably happened in 542 or 543 as the Goths marched to or from their siege of Naples. The two men met at Totila's request and sat and talked to each other for some time at the gates of the monastery.[10]

Visits of this kind were usually an ominous sign that soldiers were roamimg the countryside looking for supplies. The leaders of both armies knew the importance of dealing fairly with the local population and paying for what they took, but subordinates often treated local people badly, stealing their crops and driving away their cattle. Military requisitioning led to food shortages and famine and was a major factor in turning public opinion against one side or the other—or both.

The Goths achieved most of their victories by ambushing the imperial troops. They had less success in battles on an open plain because they never found a way of coping with their enemy's mounted bowmen, who would suddenly arrive, unleash a shower of arrows and gallop away before they could be engaged with lance or sword. The Goths also lacked an effective technique for penetrating the walls of cities where Belisarius had left garrisons; instead, they preferred to lay siege to a city and starve it into submission, a process which greatly increased the suffering of the local population.

Rome was first encircled by the Goths in March 537 and during the following months many citizens wasted away from hunger and disease. Early in 538, Belisarius was able to lift the siege by mounting a diversionary attack against the Gothic settlements on the Adriatic coast, so that many of the Goths at Rome hurried off to protect their families. A second siege (late 545 to December 546) was an even grimmer affair. Totila had the city encircled but lacked the strength to storm its walls, while Belisarius waited with his army a short way off near the coast, but was too weak to drive Totila away The military stalemate lasted a year until four members of the garrison, appalled by the suffering of the citizens, showed the Goths how to break down one of the gates and force their way into the city. There they found a population decimated by plague and starvation; even members of the aristocracy were reduced to wandering the city in rags, looking for nettles to eat. Totila gave orders that his soldiers were not to rape women or kill civilians so that the citizens were spared those further horrors.[11]

The hardships of the two sieges were an inducement to senatorial families to leave Italy and resettle in the relative peace and security of the East.[12] Eastward migration of the upper classes had been going on gradually for about a hundred years as aristocrats were enticed to Constantinople by the social life of the capital or the political opportuni-

Saint Benedict in his Community

ties of the court. The pace of resettlement increased when great Italian landowners lost touch with their overseas estates around the western Mediterranean when provinces like Spain and North Africa slipped out of the empire and into the hands of barbarian regimes. Nevertheless many great families hung on in Italy, still enormously wealthy, still emotionally attached to their ancient capital and still willing to serve the ruling power as advisers and administrators. For example, Cassiodorus, a senator and former secretary to Theoderic, returned to high office in 533 and served a succession of Gothic rulers until at least 537, possibly until the capture of Ravenna in 540.[13] Other senators lingered in Rome during the second siege, wringing their hands and unable to decide whether to throw in their lot with Belisarius or Totila. When the siege was over many of them also left for the East. The senate quickly became moribund and then disappeared altogether in the 580s.

Of course, most Italians did not have the luxury of a bolt-hole in Byzantium. Most of them 'swung with the wind' as military campaigns moved up and down the peninsula.[14] When Belisarius and his army first arrived in the extreme south of Italy, the people received him favourably, partly because Theodahad, the Gothic king at the time, was an unpopular ruler, notorious for his corruption. It was not long before goodwill towards the invaders evaporated. As the Byzantine troops moved north they impoverished the countryside by 'enthusiastic robbery', creating hostility to the imperial cause that lasted for years.[15] When they reached Naples there was a short siege followed by a massacre, led by Caucasian mercenaries in the Byzantine army, who ignored even the appeals from people who had taken refuge in churches. News of Naples' fate spread quickly. When Belisarius arrived at Rome, the citizens prudently opened the gates, though without any obvious enthusiasm, and towns to the north, such as Perugia and Spoleto, were also taken without trouble. Perhaps the best example of 'swinging with the wind' came from Ravenna, where the middling citizens—the small landowners, wealthy artisans and professional men—who had done well from serving the Gothic court, survived the short siege of the city in 540 and then adjusted smoothly to the arrival of the Byzantines. On the other hand the invasion aroused hostility elsewhere. In Rimini a detachment of Byzantine troops was welcomed into the city but then, after apparently antagonising the Italo-Roman inhabitants, was besieged by the Goths from without and attacked by the populace from within.

Fear of Gothic reprisals made people cautious in their response to Belisarius and with good reason: the Goths also had atrocities on their record, notably in Milan and Tivoli. During the second phase of the war Totila managed—usually—to keep Gothic troops under control and to cultivate public approval successfully. A substantial number of Italo-Romans joined his army and were deployed in garrison duties and other supporting roles; many slaves took up arms on his behalf, possibly because their masters

Saint Benedict in his Community

had fled or been killed and they had no other allegiance; and a steady stream of deserters from the imperial army came over to the Gothic side. During the early 540s some of the Byzantine generals were extraordinarily careless about maintaining good relations between their troops and the local population. There was rape and robbery and general lawlessness and Italians began to long for the re-establishment of Gothic rule. In the very last years of the war, when both Belisarius and Totila had left the scene, there was much casual cruelty on both sides: for example, when the Goths left Rome for the last time, they killed everyone they met on the way out and as the Byzantines advanced to take their place they killed everyone they met on the way in.

Benedict and his monks were, in a literal sense, lifted above the conflict as they followed their daily routine of prayer on their mountain top. Yet the changing fortunes of war must still have affected them. War plays havoc with trade and the community must have found that the supply of food and other necessities could cease without warning. Monks must have had to leave the monastery for lengthy periods (as in *Dialogue* 12.1 perhaps) to seek out new supplies and settle contracts with merchants. The flight of the aristocracy to the East meant the loss of powerful patrons and donors and there may have been a reduction in the size of the novitiate, since Benedict had previously recruited many monks from noble families (*Dialogue* 3.14). On the other hand, wealthy families often gave away lands or libraries before they left, so monasteries may have gained these as assets.

The community also had to respond to the human wreckage washed up on the slopes of Monte Cassino. Over the years, people came to the community in various kinds of distress, as Gregory's *Dialogue* makes clear, and it was inevitable that some of them would be refugees from the war. Benedict said that all visitors were to be welcomed 'like Christ' (*RB* 53.1), with special concern being shown to the poor. The arrangements for visitors were surprisingly elaborate: a guest house was built with its own kitchen, staffed by monks who were experienced in catering for the visitors' needs (*RB* 53.16–22). This degree of separation was necessary to prevent visitors from disturbing the community's routine, but it also suggests that people were arriving at all hours of the day and night and in numbers far greater than the categories of people—such as pilgrims and pious Christians—who might normally have been expected to visit a monastery.[16] Some of these additional people must surely have been refugees from the war; hungry, exhausted and traumatised, their presence would have been a real challenge for the community and especially for Benedict, who insisted that the abbot's place was with his guests (*RB* 56.1) and therefore with their raw emotions and urgent demands.

In addition to the terrors of war, the population was unsettled by ominous events in the natural world. There were solar eclipses in 538 and 540. In the spring of 536, and lasting for more than a year, the sky was filled with a veil of dust, 'like a tautened skin', through which the sun shone shone feebly with a strange blue light—'a most dread portent'.[17] Summer temperatures were unusually low for several years. Spectacular comets flashed across the sky, each visible for more than a month. In 537 Vesuvius rumbled and shook, and though it did not spew any ash, it terrified the people living near its base. In the east, Edessa and Tarsus were overwhelmed by floods, Antioch was twice destroyed by earthquakes, and Constantinople was rocked repeatedly.

During the 540s, Italy was swept by an epidemic, part of the first European pandemic of bubonic plague. The disease first appeared at a city in the Nile delta in July 541. From there it spread to the coastal cities of the eastern Mediterranean, reaching Constantinople in 542. It then accompanied ships' crews and cargoes to Italy, Spain and southern Gaul, arriving in 543 and moving from the coasts to the towns and villages of the interior. It is possible that the effects of the epidemic in Italy were patchy and less extensive than they had been in the east, but in some localities the death toll must have been very high.[18]

Bad weather, plague mortality and the disruption of rural life led inevitably to crop failure and famine. Needy people came to Monte Cassino begging for food and Benedict's community gave away everything they had in store. Gregory's *Dialogue* refers to a famine in Campania (*Dialogue* 21.1 and 28.1) and a likely date for this would be 537, when the province was suffering a crop failure caused by the dust veil of the previous year and military requisitioning carried out by the agents of Belisarius. The whole of central Italy from coast to coast was stricken with famine in 538–9. Some crops were sown but were left unattended so that they did not germinate; others grew but had nobody to harvest them; people were forced out of their homes and into the hills where they lived on acorns and berries; diseases of malnutrition were rife; and there were even cases of cannibalism. There were food shortages again in many parts of Italy in 543–4.

The war was a disaster for Italy and for the Roman empire. Justinian may have congratulated himself on winning a victory—at last—but he had squandered the financial surplus he inherited from his predecessors, ruined Italy as a source of revenue, and left the empire more divided than ever. The war did more to undermine the social order in Italy than Gothic rule had ever done. It drove people away from their farms and into fortified towns and contributed, in some parts of the country, to a collapse of rural life that lasted for more than a hundred years. This was the turbulent and depressing background to Benedict's message of stability and peace.

3

Religious Life under Gothic Rule

THE GOTHS' RESILIENCE through the years of war came from their sense of community, which was nurtured, in part, by their religion, a variety of Christianity known as Arianism. Did the Goths' religious identity harden into antagonism towards the Catholics around them? Was this a factor that contributed to nearly twenty years of warfare?[1] These questions need to be considered if we are to understand the religious and political background to Benedict's life.

The Arianism of the Goths was a survival from the great religious controversy of the fourth century over the relationship between God the Father and God the Son. Most Christians considered that the matter had been settled by the Council of Nicaea in 325, which declared that Father and Son were co-eternal and con-substantial, but Arians continued to insist that the Son, though still to some extent divine, was later and lesser than the Father and similar, rather than identical, in substance. Arian ideas had been largely confined to the fringes of the Christian world, chiefly to the Germanic tribes of the Danube basin, but when those tribes moved into the western Mediterranean and became the ruling powers in North Africa, Spain, Gaul and Italy, Arianism once again became a challenge to orthodox Christians. In the Roman province of North Africa, which was conquered by the Vandals in the 430s, there was active persecution of Catholics by the new regime and many Church people were driven into exile. There was also milder persecution at the hands of the Visigoths in some parts of Gaul.

In Italy, on the other hand, an accommodation gradually developed between these two Christian creeds. When Gothic tribesmen were recruited into the Roman army, the Romans recognised that those troops and their families would want to worship according to the customs of their Arian forefathers. A special dispensation to this effect was agreed by the councils of the Church and incorporated into Roman civil law. Arian churches began to appear in centres of Gothic settlement such as Milan, Pavia and Spoleto; in Ravenna, where there may have been as many as seven; and in Rome, where there were three, notably the church now known as Sant' Agata dei Goti, built probably early in the fifth century and endowed with mosaics in the 460s by Ricimer, the leading Gothic general and strongman of the time.

Benedict might, as an inquisitive young student, have visited Sant' Agata, curious to see the differences between Catholic liturgy and iconography and those of the Arians. He is unlikely to have seen anything that surprised him. Sant' Agata had a columned nave with side aisles, much like the other churches

Religious Life under Gothic Rule

of Rome, and an apse with mosaics of Christ holding an open book and flanked by the twelve apostles, led by Peter and Paul, the two martyrs on whom Rome's primacy as a religious centre depended. The mosaics did not differ in design from orthodox iconography and they remained untouched when Gregory the Great rededicated the church in 592.[2] Much the same was true of the church of Sant' Apollinare Nuovo in Ravenna, founded by Theoderic, decorated during his reign, and intended as his court chapel—and therefore a building where, more than anywhere else, one might expect to find examples of 'Arian art', if such a thing existed. But two series of mosaics in the church, depicting the life and passion of Christ in ways that might have had Arian connotations, were left untouched when the church was renovated and rededicated after the Goths had left, showing that these depictions of Christ were perfectly acceptable to Catholics.[3]

Just as the layout of Arian and Catholic churches was similar, so, it seems, was the worship that went on in them. Half a century earlier, the Arian bishop Maximinus had visited a Catholic church in Milan and been astonished to discover that there was little difference between his own liturgy and that of the Catholics; they 'appear to give the same baptism, the same sacrament of the body and blood of Christ', he wrote, and they 'likewise honour the Apostles and Martyrs'.[4] Arians and Catholics had worshipped together occasionally during the fifth century and it is possible that this continued in small towns and other places where there were no significant social or political repercussions from doing so. In about 500 the Church authorities in southern Gaul issued instructions that clergy were not to pray or chant psalms with heretics, which is almost certainly a sign that that is exactly what they had been doing. Even then, the Church's disapproval of Arians was not very profound; Arian converts were easily received into the Church by the simple laying-on of hands and in 511 the Council of Orleans decided that Arian clergy could make the switch in the same way and be assigned at once to any Catholic church that the local bishop wished. As far as most of the population were concerned, 'in usual church practice and people's everyday lives, there can scarcely have been much to distinguish Arians from Catholics'.[5]

Another point of convergence between the two creeds was the Goths' emphasis on scripture. During Theoderic's reign, scholars were revising the text of the Gothic Bible, moving towards a slightly less literal and more idiomatic translation from the original Greek. In the process ideas were borrowed from the Latin Bible. As the Latin Bible was itself undergoing revision during these years, it is not impossible that Catholic scholars also picked up ideas from their Gothic counterparts.

The Goths did not accept the Catholic position on Christ's divinity because they said that arguments about divine substance, such as those that had taken place at Nicaea, were unscriptural. The Bible had made it clear, in their eyes, that the Father was the God

Religious Life under Gothic Rule

of the Son and that Jesus himself had demonstrated this. 'The Goths assert that the Father is greater than the Son', wrote the early Church historian Theodoret, 'but they refuse to describe the Son as a creature'.[6] They saw the Son as 'the only-begotten God', as a creator and mediator, 'a Son so great and so good, so powerful, so wise, so full' that it was right to glorify and adore him. This reverence for Jesus is illustrated at Sant' Apollinare Nuovo, a church originally dedicated to 'the Lord Jesus Christ': for example, one of the icons suggests that Jesus was seen as a creator existing before human time and one of the mosaics depicts Him as the Eternal Judge, flanked by angels and separating sheep from goats. The Arian baptistery has a mosaic depicting the baptism of Jesus in the same way as the mosaic in the nearby Catholic baptistery, which had been built a few years earlier. In practice, therefore, the significance of Jesus for the Goths may have meant that the theological differences between them and Catholics may not have been difficult to gloss over, particularly if the liturgy of the Gothic churches offered no challenge to orthodoxy.

We can certainly assume that Benedict rejected Arian theology. But did he go further than this? It has been suggested that he took up the cudgels on behalf of orthodoxy in a campaign of 'militant anti-Arianism' and that this is reflected in the *Rule*. It is a striking fact that nowhere in the *Rule* can the name 'Jesus' be found; instead, Benedict always uses the words 'Christ', 'Lord' or 'King'. This is no coincidence. Benedict cuts short biblical quotations in order to exclude the name 'Jesus', and he downplays details of Jesus's ministry. It has been suggested that Benedict was trying to emphasise the divinity of Jesus as a counter to the Arianism of the Goths, who supposedly emphasised Jesus's humanity.[7]

Leaving aside the question of whether a monastic rule would have been an appropriate vehicle for a militant campaign, it is important to note that, in the Christological debates of Benedict's time, it was common to use the term 'Christ' to denote the whole reality of the Word made flesh, encompassing both its divine nature and its human nature. Benedict was probably trying to avoid tilting his Christology towards either of the natures. In any case, it seems unlikely that Benedict and his contemporaries in central and southern Italy were bothered very much by Goths and Arianism. There were relatively few Goths living round about and the possibility of conversion and assimilation was demonstrated by the fact that a Goth—presumably a Catholic convert—came to join the monks at Subiaco and was warmly received (*Dialogue* 6.1).

The religious policy of the Ostrogothic kings was tolerant and non-interventionist—quite the opposite of the Arian Vandal rulers in North Africa. Theoderic himself was an Arian, but there were Catholics in his immediate family, in his court and elsewhere in the Gothic community. He made it clear early in his reign that he would leave the Church to settle its own affairs and would protect its rights and property. This was the basis of the good relationship that normally existed between him and the Church leaders. Pope Gelasius (492–6) referred to him as 'a most excellent man, my son King Theoderic'. When Theoderic visited Rome in 500 he is said to have gone into St Peter's 'most devoutly and like a Catholic'. It would be unfair to think that this was just a charade; he seems genuinely to have thought that religious belief was a personal matter and should be respected. He once told the Jews of Genoa: 'I cannot command your faith, for no one is forced to believe against his will'.[8] Theoderic was proud of his Gothic religion and endowed it handsomely, but he refused to prevent the conversion of other Goths to Catholicism. Theoderic's own Arianism was therefore not an issue. The popes were much more likely to pin the label of 'heretic' on to the emperor in Constantinople than on to the king in Ravenna. For most of Benedict's lifetime the pope was at loggerheads with the emperor over the latter's meddling in ecclesiastical politics and his compromises with the Monophysite theology that was popular in the East. At home in Italy, the popes were concerned far more with heresies like Manichaeism than they were with Arianism.[9] When Pope Hormisdas (514–23) discovered Manichaean cells in Rome he had the heretics' books gathered up and burnt in front of the Lateran, something he never did to the Arians. Indeed, throughout these years an Arian church remained open in Rome without giving offence to Catholics, even to someone as sternly orthodox as Gelasius. It would seem that peaceful

Saint Benedict in his Community

coexistence was really the norm in relations between Arians and Catholics.

However, in the last years of his life, Theoderic's relationship with the Catholic Church became tetchy. The source of his irritation was the looming crisis over the succession to his throne and Theoderic's failure to get everyone to agree on the next ruler's identity. Factions began to form in Rome and Ravenna, including one that pressed for a revival of Gothic values. The imperial authorities in Constantinople were unhelpful and Justinian inflamed the situation by attacking the small Arian community there, closing churches and forcibly converting their congregations. Theoderic demolished a Catholic chapel outside Verona, apparently as a reprisal, and he had Boethius, the philosopher and leading senator, imprisoned and then executed, which was also interpreted as an anti-Catholic move.[10] In 526 he sent the current pope, John I, on a mission to Constantinople to persuade Justinian to reverse his policies but the pope failed to secure all Theoderic's objectives and on his return to Ravenna Theoderic put him under house arrest, where he unfortunately died. This immediately gave rise to rumours of ill-treatment and John was hailed as a martyr; in fact, it is much more likely that the pope, who was already old and frail, was simply worn out by his long journey.

It was rumoured that Theoderic, in the very last days of his life, issued an order for Goths to take over Catholic churches. There is no evidence to corroborate the rumour; in any case, such a policy seems inherently unlikely, given Theoderic's long policy of religious toleration and the number of influential Catholics at his court. Such a policy would probably have needed detachments of Gothic troops to be sent far and wide across Italy in support, moves that would have been militarily suicidal. If the closure of churches had been ordered at all, it may have been meant for Ravenna alone. Theoderic had been on bad terms with the local Catholics. They had been behind a riot against Ravenna's Jews in 519, during which a synagogue had been burned down, and Theoderic had forced the Catholics to pay compensation for it. The Ravenna bishops were also very pushy, hoping to inflate their diocese into a new patriarchate to stand alongside those in Constantinople, Alexandria and elsewhere.

The forces behind the events of Theoderic's last years were essentially political, not religious. The outpouring of public grief that followed the death of John did not translate into a wave of anti-Arianism. The popes who served under the Ostrogothic kings, from Gelasius to Silverius (536–7),[11] never found Arianism an obstacle to cooperating with the court in Ravenna. A case in point was Agapitus (535–6), who was outspoken about the errors of Arian belief but went to Constantinople on King Theodahad's behalf to try to persuade Justinian to call off the invasion of Italy. It was not until Vigilius became pope in 537, a creature of the imperial court placed on his throne by Justinian's soldiers, that Arianism was offered as a justification for conflict with the Goths.

The war in Italy was not an eruption of religious conflict from within; it was a war of reconquest from without, launched by Justinian. It was possible for Justinian to persuade himself that he had a religious motive in doing so; he sincerely believed that the Roman emperor provided religious as well as political leadership and that his personal rule was a guarantee of doctrinal orthodoxy. This was not, however, a justification which he offered in the immediate prelude to the invasion of Italy; his military adventures were part of a larger project to recover all the lands once subject to the ancient Romans. Searching for a pretext to invade, he tried to pick a fight with Queen Amalasuntha, but the Arianism of her Gothic people was not one of the complaints he laid against her. He got one of his ambassadors to frighten Theodahad into surrender, but the deal made between them said nothing about religion. When Belisarius arrived at the gates of Naples he told the inhabitants that he had come to secure their freedom in a war against slavery—again, no word about religion—which was an explanation he offered many times in the following years, usually bolstered by the charge that Theoderic's kingship had been illegitimate from the start.[12] Justinian never claimed to be defending Italian Catholics against Arians. Indeed, the Goths' religion was scarcely ever mentioned, their churches were not burnt, their priests were not executed, and victories over them were not celebrated with religious triumphalism.

Religious Life under Gothic Rule

On the Gothic side there was no obvious animosity towards Catholics. During the siege of Rome in 537, worship continued in the usual way in St Peter's and St Paul's, even though St Paul's was some way outside the city walls and open to Gothic attack.[13] Later in 537, when the ranks of both armies had been depleted by casualties and famine, the Goths sent ambassadors to Belisarius to propose an honourable compromise — which Belisarius spurned — and in the course of the negotiations, the ambassadors pointed out that the Goths had scrupulously respected Catholic churches and religious practices and never interfered when Arians converted to Catholicism, points which Belisarius was unable to deny.[14] Religious toleration seems to have continued in the following decade; Totila was respectful towards the Church and punished its priests and bishops only when they involved themselves in political and military matters.

Generally speaking, the Church and the papacy were not very much bothered by Gothic Arianism. Heresy it might be, but it was heresy they could live with. Arian theology made no claim to universal validity and the Arian community, through its steady trickle of conversions to Catholicism, was on the way to assimilation and extinction. It is difficult to see why Benedict, too, should have been bothered by Arianism. It is very unlikely that the blatant politicisation of Arian-Catholic relations by Justinian, Vigilius and others would have made him revise his opinion. He is much more likely to have accepted that Arians were mistaken in some aspects of their belief about God and Jesus but that peaceful coexistence between the two faiths should continue.

4

Benedict as a Student

THE FIRST PAGE of the *Dialogue* tells us that the young Benedict was sent from his home to Rome for higher education (*Dialogue* intro. 1). Provincial elites normally sent their sons to the higher schools between the ages of 14 and 17, so Benedict might have arrived in Rome in the mid-490s.

The Rome of Benedict's day was much reduced in size and splendour from the imperial capital of the past. The population had fallen from about 500,000 in 450 to perhaps as little as 100,000. It seems to have grown again during the peaceful conditions of Theoderic's reign, but some districts within the walls were now quietly reverting to scrub and pasture; even close to the city centre there were roofless buildings, their walls collapsed, their rooms filled with rubbish, their fabric torn apart as stone and marble were re-cycled to other structures. Yet the local elite were still enormously proud of their city; it was 'a marvel', they said, a 'wonderful forest of buildings'.[1] They still met in the Senate House, which they had plans to refurbish, and they carefully preserved the ancient Forum, with its historic facades and statues. During Benedict's time, part of the outer circuit of the Colosseum was dismantled and rebuilt to make good the damage done by an earthquake. Other restoration projects were launched in Theoderic's reign, including repairs to the enormous Baths of Caracalla.

The great houses of the city's elite were now less numerous than they had been at the height of the empire. They were still places of astonishing magnificence; it was said that they were little towns within the city, with squares, fountains, places of worship and different kinds of baths. In addition to the owner's family, they accommodated hundreds of servants and received a daily stream of visitors. The main feature of the fifth-century urban villa was a columned reception hall—a place for doing business, hosting dinner parties and providing entertainment—often with a library alongside, where, in addition to the family's precious collection of books, the householder would gather his friends for discussions on political or religious topics. However, some elite families had fallen on hard times or moved away to Constantinople and there were now depressing ruins on the once-fashionable slopes of the Esquiline Hill.

The most conspicuous new developments in the city were taking place under papal auspices: the greatest of these, the enormous church of S. Maria Maggiore, had been built in the 440s, its classical columns and its mosaics of Christ and the apostles dressed in togas a symptom of the way that old traditions were blending into a Christian future. The city's elite had gradually become involved in this process. From the 390s onwards, more than twenty churches had been built in various parts of the city, mainly with money donated by wealthy lay people and mainly in districts where the donors' families were powerful. So much aristocratic largesse had been expended on these efforts that the pope and his officials began to fret about the amount of Church property and the number of religious and charitable activities that were under elite patronage and were not under central ecclesiastical control.

Most of Rome's citizens lived in large apartment blocks (*insulae*), where dwellings of various sizes mingled with shops and workshops. There would have been taverns here and there, offering wine, fast food, raucous company and prostitutes. Some of the *insulae* were falling into disrepair, driving their inhabitants into the middle floors of the building where they were relatively safe both from leaking roofs and periodic floods. In the abandoned villas of the elite the slaves and servants stayed on in their quarters, squatters came in to colonise and subdivide the family's rooms and cattle might be stabled in the reception halls. There were, however, enough members of the elite — still with extraordinary wealth — to continue many of the traditions of civic organisation and patronage. Most of the population were dependent on them in some way: as tenants, as slaves, as clients in the city's food-distribution system, or as day-labourers working on construction sites or hauling goods from the banks of the Tiber to granaries and store-houses. The elite stepped in to ensure the continuation of services that had once been provided by the emperor: the imperial baths, for instance, which were huge leisure parks where anyone could dip in the hot and cold pools—oblivious, apparently, to the filth in the water—exert themselves in an exercise yard, relax in a garden, carry on an affair or read in a library. The elite also funded public games and displays. The Colosseum was the venue for spectacular shows, often involving fights with wild animals. However, the Colosseum had become less fashionable than the Circus Maximus, where people flocked to watch chariot racing, with the added excitement of confrontations between the gangs of supporters that gathered around the charioteers.

The young Benedict was probably sent to Rome to board with relatives or a patron of the family and to be enrolled with a reputable tutor. Gregory tells us that Benedict had a 'liberal education' (*Dialogue* intro. 1). Such an education had a well-defined content, which Gregory would have known, and we must therefore assume that his choice of words was deliberate and accurate. Liberal education consisted of the three verbal arts—grammar, dialectic and rhetoric—followed by the numerical arts of arithmetic, geometry, astronomy and music. The order of these studies might vary somewhat from school to school, but grammar was always the starting point. The numerical arts always came last; in fact, Benedict may not have stayed in Rome long enough to grapple with them. The study of grammar involved the ana-

Benedict as a Student

lysis of syllables, words, syntax and style, with the aim of learning how language should logically be understood. A word-by-word analysis of a text might also, in the hands of a skilful grammarian, introduce the student to history, geography and many other branches of general knowledge. The aim of dialectic was to develop logical reasoning; the numerical arts were supposed to promote abstract thought. In rhetoric, the student had to argue one side of a case—revolving around some problematic, even improbable, issue—using not only the conventions of oratory, but drawing on historical analogies, moral values and a sense of justice and the law, inspired still by the speeches of Cicero, now 500 years in the past. Whatever the artificiality of the curriculum, it provided the bureaucracies of the time with a supply of 'shrewd and active minds'.[2] As for Benedict's religious education, it can be assumed that he learnt the Bible at home in Nursia, but he cannot have had a programme of formal religious instruction in Rome. No such programme existed; the Church did not provide one, and nobody drew up a curriculum of that kind until Cassiodorus did so in the 560s.

On the other hand, there can be no doubt that Benedict's curriculum was steeped in the ideas of pre-Christian—and therefore pagan—Latin writers. The works of Virgil and Cicero were foundational texts for the study of grammar and rhetoric respectively; Ovid, Horace, Livy and others were also studied by generations of students. Valerius Maximus had written a compendium of behaviour, both virtuous and vicious, arranged under various headings, and this was often quoted in rhetorical debates. Marcus Terentius Varro had gathered all the knowledge of his day (first century BCE) into an encyclopaedic corpus of about seventy books in 600 volumes and these were quarried by later writers, including Augustine. Varro was a particular influence on Maurus Servius Honoratus and Martianus Capella, two of the most important grammarians of the fifth century, whose books were circulating in Rome in Benedict's student days. Writers in the old tradition were now reflecting in their works the more eclectic culture of the fifth century. Martianus, for example, imagined the liberal arts as bridesmaids of Philology, who was about to rise to heaven to be married to Mercury, the god of Eloquence. This literary device allowed Martianus not only to describe each of the arts, but to argue that the human soul can rise from the body 'through the exercise of its intellect' and to depict the old Olympian gods as intermediaries between humanity and Jupiter, the father of all things and a 'sacred intellect'.[3] All of this was still a very long way from a Christian conception of salvation or of the divine, but it may have helped people to embrace the new beliefs without feeling that they were entirely rejecting the old.

Christian readers began to find fresh meanings in old texts. Virgil's poetry was full of delphic statements that were open to reinterpretation. Perhaps the most intriguing of them was in the poet's fourth

Eclogue, where he had written: 'The First Born of the New Age is already on his way from high heaven down to earth'.[4] Speculation about this verse continued intermittently for centuries. Editing copies of classical poetry and writing commentaries on them was a common activity among the Christian leisured classes.

Another celebrated text, pregnant with various interpretations, was a passage at the end of Cicero's *Republic*, where Cicero imagined a dream experienced by the Roman statesman and victorious general, Scipio Africanus the Younger. Scipio finds himself in a lofty starlit place, looking down on the planets revolving in their orbits, with the earth a tiny motionless sphere at the bottom of the universe. The ghost of his long-dead grandfather warns Scipio that, in the larger scheme of things, worldly renown is but limited and transient, and one should act in ways that help to release the soul to a higher realm. Cicero's description of this dream was the subject of a long and influential commentary by Ambrosius Theodosius Macrobius, probably written about 410 and circulating in Rome at the time Benedict was a student there. Macrobius saw this as an opportunity to explain the views of Plotinus and other Neoplatonists on the nature of the One and the soul's relation to it. Young Romans would certainly have been advised to read the 'Dream'; it was regarded as one of the very finest examples of Latin prose, a passage of almost poetic intensity, and in Macrobius's edition they would have found much to reflect upon,

Saint Benedict in his Community

however committed they already might have been to Christianity. Cicero was almost certainly an influence on Gregory's description of Benedict's vision of a brilliant ray of light, seen from a monastery window on Monte Cassino (*Dialogue* 35.2–3).[5]

A different perspective on the classics came from the cento, a poem made up of a patchwork of phrases from a famous author reassembled to create a new work with a new theme. An example of this was the cento written by Proba, an aristocratic Roman lady of the fourth century, who pieced together verses from Virgil to form an epic in which the Creation and Fall, as described in Genesis, were contrasted with the main events in the life of Christ, as described in the Gospels. Proba took considerable liberties with her biblical sources; for example, instead of having the Blessed Virgin take refuge in Egypt during the massacre of the Holy Innocents, she has her hiding in Bethlehem with the infant Jesus pressed to her bosom; instead of setting the Last Supper in an upper room, she has the disciples recumbent, Roman-style, in a grassy place; and she replaces the Beatitudes with a stern warning against striking a parent or withholding charity from the poor. It is easy to condemn the cento as plagiarism, but it must have required a close knowledge of literary and biblical sources and no little skill in bending them both to a new purpose. The result was certainly graphic. Proba's poem was widely circulated and much admired. It was adopted as a school text and came to be regarded as one of the 'apocryphal scriptures'.[6]

Benedict as a Student

Another significant author, widely read and discussed in Benedict's time, was Sedulius, whose lengthy poem, the *Carmen Paschale*, written around 440, retold the story of the gospels with a special emphasis on the miracles of Christ. Sedulius was writing for an audience that found the existing translations of the Bible rather plain, so he set out to entice his readers with a more consciously literary style. There are many echoes of Virgil and much use of paradox and allegory. In his account of the Nativity, Sedulius stressed Christ's divinity, but also aspects of his humility such as his taking the form of a slave (echoing Phil 2:7) and his identity with shepherds and lambs. Sedulius did not shrink from major theological issues: he asserted the perpetual virginity of Mary and plunged into the contemporary controversy over the nature of Christ. Sedulius's poem was enormously popular and influential. A new edition of it was prepared in Rome only a year or two before Benedict's arrival there and it was soon to be mentioned with 'conspicuous praise' in the *Decretum Gelasianum*'s list of recommended books.

Other poets were also putting the Christian message into verse as compositions which could be read for pleasure as well as for confirmation of one's faith: there was Prudentius, the Spanish poet, and Paulinus, a senatorial aristocrat and former provincial governor, who retired to a country estate at Nola in Campania where he established one of the earliest ascetic communities in Italy. Some of their poems were also used as hymns, which had recently been introduced into Church liturgy and which Benedict would later include in the Offices at Monte Cassino.[7] Benedict would almost certainly have known the poems Paulinus wrote in the traditional hexameters, with many echoes of Virgil and Horace, but using biblical characters as ideal types rather than the Olympian gods.

By the time that Benedict came to Rome, members of the educated elite had become quite relaxed about having pagan and Christian ideas alongside each other in their intellectual universe. They prepared new editions of Sedulius, as well as of Virgil and Horace, Martianus and Macrobius; they met to discuss the relationship between Christian writers such as Augustine and pagans such as Varro; and they had Christian and pagan books alongside each other on their shelves. They continued to value the moral sense of traditional culture, its balance and restraint and its pervasive order, which they could now attribute to a Christian God.

In earlier days, many educated Romans would have been able to read Greek, but by the fifth century the knowledge of that language had declined very seriously in most parts of the Latin West. It was still taught a little in cities like Rome and Milan, and used occasionally in aristocratic families with ties to the East, so it is not entirely impossible that Benedict had a smattering of it, though it is unlikely. Nevertheless, Greek ideas, now circulating in Latin translations, continued to be an essential part of the intellectual currency of the Roman world. Boethius, for example,

Benedict as a Student

was concerned to apply Aristotelian logic to Christian thought and had plans to translate the entire writings of Aristotle into Latin, showing that there was an appetite in Italy for literature of that kind.

The need for communication between the Greek and Latin worlds was shown by the arrival in Rome of Dionysius Exiguus. He was a Scythian monk who had been invited to the city by Pope Gelasius because of his exceptional fluency in both languages. His official task was to collect and edit the canon law produced over the centuries by the various councils of the Church, held in both East and West. Dionysius was also an extremely charismatic personality and in the cultured circles of Rome he must have made quite a splash; he displayed 'in his own deeds the righteousness about which he had read in the books of the Lord ... He had great simplicity coupled with wisdom, humility coupled with learning [and among] other excellent qualities he had this unusual virtue, namely, not to despise taking part in conversations with the laity'.[8] Years later, Benedict drew upon Dionysius's work when writing his *Rule*; some of his turns of phrase can be attributed to one or other of Dionysius's writings. Benedict would certainly have known Dionysius by reputation and although it is pure speculation to suggest that he met him or heard him speak, that is not altogether impossible—in a city of Rome's modest size, news of a gifted speaker would have travelled quickly. It would have been natural, when Benedict was working on the *Rule* and seeking support for some of his ideas, to turn to the writings of a person he knew and admired. The character and lifestyle of Dionysius may even have been the example that encouraged Benedict to set out on a monastic life after his departure from Rome.

Throughout the fifth century, the most important corpus of Greek ideas was Neoplatonism, which was known through the writings of Plotinus, Porphyry and others. Most people probably encountered these ideas piecemeal, were attracted by some, and only later came to realise that others were difficult to square with Christian belief. Plotinus's concept of a transcendent God—the One, ineffable and prior to all things—had obvious appeal, as did his idea of the individual soul freeing itself from the body and rising to ultimate union with the One. The problem, as Augustine realised, was to explain how the soul's progress could be made available to everyone. This was the bone of his contention with the writings of Porphyry, Plotinus's pupil. For Augustine, the soul's progress was assured by the Word made flesh and the mediation of Christ. Porphyry, however, rejected the idea of the divinity of Christ, wrote many polemics against it, and continued to see value in some of the old pagan and magical practices, which he thought could be given allegorical interpretations. In spite of these differences, Augustine had a deep and continuing respect for the 'Platonists', as he called them, for representing, more than any other thinkers, 'the closest approximation to our Christian position'.[9]

Benedict as a Student

Augustine towered above other Christian writers through the sheer quantity of his output, his range of interests and the quality of his thought and literary style.[10] Within a year of his death he was hailed by the pope as one of the greatest of Christian teachers. His writings were edited into collections of snippets, known as florilegia, or reproduced as extracts in the form of questions and answers to thorny biblical and doctrinal issues. It is very likely that Benedict first encountered Augustine's thought in this form rather than by reading the original works.[11]

Benedict therefore found himself in a very eclectic intellectual environment during his student days, able to read Virgil and Cicero, Proba and Porphyry, the Bible and Augustine. It may be that this was reflected years later in the reasonable tone of the *Rule* and Benedict's advice to his monks to listen to juniors and strangers and be open to shafts of wisdom from unexpected quarters. The young Benedict had learnt how to learn—'learnedly ignorant and wisely uninstructed' was Gregory's assessment (*Dialogue* intro. 1)—and this may have been the intellectual preparation he needed to write a *Rule* that was notable as a synthesis of monastic practice from different traditions.

The *Rule* begins by commanding the monks 'to listen to the instructions of your Master' (*RB* prol. 1) and ends by urging them to read the words of the Bible and the Fathers of the Church (*RB* 73). Much of the monastic day was taken up with private reading or listening to others reading—during the Offices, at mealtimes or before Compline—or listening to the teaching of the abbot or prior. Listening was to be done with 'the ear of the heart', for the aim of this instruction was to increase a monk's devotion to the Lord's service. At the same time, the heart could not be separated from the mind, as Benedict makes clear. The readings at Vigils were to include explanations of scripture from reputable commentators (RB 9.8); the readings at mealtimes might well raise questions that the abbot would need to answer (RB 38.9); and no monk was allowed to read to the assembled brethren unless he could do so with understanding (RB 38.12).

Benedict gave the intellectual life of his monks a high priority. When a monk joined the community he was given a stylus and writing tablets (RB 55.19) so that he could copy down passages from books to meditate upon or memorise.[12] Over and over again Benedict stresses the importance, not just of reading, but of being free from distractions while reading, so that each reader could give full attention to a text (RB 48.18). Monks had specified periods for 'prayerful reading',[13] at other times they were allowed to read privately while resting on their beds, and on Sundays everyone was to read or study. Seniors were to patrol the monastery to make sure that monks were not neglecting their reading or distracting others. In Lent each monk was to be given a book from the monastic library to read 'through from the beginning' (RB 48.15). Most reading probably focused on short passages—either from a book or from the monk's own tablets—which a monk would read slowly and repeatedly, savouring the words, perhaps committing some of them to memory, and allowing his meditations to transform themselves into prayer. At other times—as when reading florilegia—the approach would be more didactic. The Lenten book that was read straight through, whether it was biblical or not, was an opportunity for the reader to see the whole shape of an author's argument or description of events.

The books of those days were normally written in a continuous script with no breaks between the words and it was easier for a reader to identify each word individually if he whispered the text quietly to himself. As a result, Benedict found it necessary to remind the monks that if they wished to read in the dormitory, they should be careful not to disturb their neighbours (RB 48.5). Looking beyond the words, a reader had to recognise how an argument was developing from sentence to sentence and how the sentences might be grouped into paragraphs to create the association of ideas that the author had intended. Whereas the modern reader can run an eye over a page while thinking of something else entirely, the reader of Benedict's day was engaged in constant mental editing.

What did the monks read? There can be absolutely no doubt that a thorough knowledge of the Bible was their first priority. Their aim must have been to make the Bible so completely their own that the words of scripture flowed naturally into their thoughts and seamlessly into their conversation, just as they did into Benedict's writing of the *Rule*. This also had a practical purpose. The light in the oratory was so poor that psalms and canticles would, of necessity, have been chanted from memory and some scripture readings also had to be recited by heart (e.g., *RB* 9.10 and 10.2). It is not surprising that Benedict was critical of mistakes made in the oratory (*RB* 45) for this was a sign, not just of carelessness, but of inadequate knowledge of the scriptures.

Some commentators believe that Benedict required his monks to read the Bible and little else. They argue that since the Bible was normally transcribed and bound into a number of separate volumes, it could be regarded as a library (*bibliotheca*) in itself, and therefore the references in the *Rule* to 'the library' and to 'books' (for example, at *RB* 48.15) are really no more than references to the Bible and its individual volumes. It is true that a few early Christian writers, notably Jerome, did refer to the Bible as a *bibliotheca*, but there is not much evidence that this had become a common usage that Benedict was likely to copy.[14] Benedict's own cultural background—that of the Roman senatorial aristocracy and provincial elite— was full of books and libraries and it is far more likely that Benedict used the word *bibliotheca* in its ordinary sense as a repository of books.[15]

The use of *bibliotheca* to refer to the Bible was, of course, a metaphor which paid tribute to the richness and diversity of the biblical canon. It might also describe the diversity of texts on the pages which a

Benedict as a Student

monk held in his hands. These were bound together into a codex, the precursor of the modern book, made up of pages of papyrus or parchment, written on both sides, with a spine down one edge. The layout of text on the page of a codex left margins on which notes could be written and it was possible for blank pages to be inserted for longer comments. Published commentaries on a text could be bound with the text itself in the same volume.[16] For example, a monk picking up the Book of Genesis might find that, in addition to the biblical text, he had parts of the commentaries of Basil and Jerome, some florilegia of Augustine, some marginal references to Origen and possibly the jottings of his abbot all bound together in the one volume. In this sense, therefore, a codex of part of the scriptures might be a *bibliotheca* between two covers. Indeed, it has been suggested that the term codex/codices might be a kind of library classification signifying a body of literature on a particular subject.[17] If the word *bibliotheca* is applied to codices of this kind it does not narrow the monks' reading to the biblical text alone; on the contrary, it enlarges it from the Bible to the commentaries and background material that were bound with it.

Because every book was copied by scribes, every copy could be littered with errors. A reader with a new book would usually try to borrow another copy from a friend and compare the two in the hope of reconstructing an accurate version of the original. Presumably, over the years, the monastery's books were progressively edited in this way, but it was something the monks would have needed to attempt every time a new book was acquired; certainly, every new copy of the Bible would have had to be carefully proof-read. It was becoming customary by this time for bibles to have notes of many different kinds inserted, not just textual corrections but chapter headings, marginalia and cross-references to commentaries. A diligent reader would have wanted to put other volumes alongside his Bible and would have needed a table or desk with sufficient space to do this. He would also have needed a surface on which to spread out his wax tablets and write down the passages he wanted to use for meditation.

Bearing all this in mind, we can begin to imagine what the library at Monte Cassino might have been like. It would have been much less than the great monastic libraries of the Middle Ages, but also more than a cupboard full of books. It was probably a modest room with good natural light, opening on to a short colonnade or portico and furnished like the Church libraries of Rome, with a couple of desks, a chair and a lectern, and several cupboards for books and records. The library was not really a place for extensive reading—the whispering of texts would have been too distracting—but it would have been an active reference library, a place for looking things up and copying things down.

What books are likely to have been in the library? Benedict urged his monks to follow 'the doctrines of the holy Fathers', to attend to every page of the Old and New Testaments and to read the books of the holy catholic Fathers of the Church (*RB* 73.2–4). This bracketing of the Bible with the Fathers was typical of the theological climate of the time. The great doctrinal controversies that revolved around the Church councils of Ephesus and Chalcedon could no longer be resolved by a reference to scripture alone; the explanations offered by the great theologians of the Church became equally important points of reference and achieved canonical authority in their own right.[18] Florilegia were compiled from them. Particular veneration was given to those Fathers, men like Athanasius, Ambrose and Hilary of Poitiers, who had defended the Council of Nicaea against heretical deviations, or men like Cyril of Alexandria who had been influential at Ephesus and Chalcedon. There was a huge output of florilegia in the early sixth century. These came mainly from the Greek-speaking East, with Cyril being the Father most frequently quoted, but Latin translations of them began to be available in Italy from the 520s. It is highly likely that florilegia of the Fathers were in the library at Monte Cassino.

Benedict particularly recommended the monastic writings of Basil and Cassian and the accounts of the monks of the Egyptian desert (*RB* 73.5), but these were still only some of the volumes that his community might find valuable. The list in *RB* 73 was certainly not meant to be comprehensive. For example, between supper and Compline there was a reading from Cassian or the Lives of the Desert Fathers, or 'some other work which will edify the hearers' (*RB*

42.3) and these un-named books must also have been in the library, since it would have been ridiculous to have read them aloud to the whole community and then denied individual monks the chance of studying them in private. It would be very surprising if the library did not also contain copies of Proba and Sedulius, Prudentius and Paulinus, the biographies of St Antony and St Martin and at least some of the accounts of the apostles and martyrs. It is reasonable to assume that the library kept copies of the Church histories by Eusebius and Socrates Scholasticus. The text of the *Rule* suggests that Benedict had access to the works of Cyprian, Origen, Ambrose, Jerome and others, and especially to Augustine. If Augustine's works were in the library and the monks were encouraged to consult them, their intellectual horizons may have become very wide indeed.

There are no echoes of the old pagan literature in the *Rule* but some, at least, of the Latin classics must have been in the monastery library. Young boys who were dedicated to a monastic life by their parents (*RB* 59.1) would have needed a basic education in grammar and writing and the monk who gave it to them would probably have done no more than regurgitate the education he himself had received, in which case Quintilian, Cicero and others would have found a place on the library shelves. Some of the Latin classics retained a value as reference works: Livy's encyclopaedic *Natural History*, books by Varro, monographs on food and horticulture and medical texts by Galen. Among the classics generally, it is

Benedict as a Student

difficult to believe that an old favourite like Virgil would have been entirely dismissed. In the more relaxed cultural atmosphere of Benedict's lifetime it was possible to concede that the old secular education had a contribution to make to Christian understanding. Augustine encouraged this view by showing his admiration for the characters of many of the pagan philosophers with whom he disagreed and Cassiodorus wrote that 'both in the Bible and in the most learned commentaries we understand a great deal through figures of speech, through definitions, through grammar, rhetoric, dialectic' and so on and knowledge of these matters 'is useful and not to be avoided'. Rather than 'confining' his monks to the Bible and a few of the works of the Fathers, it is much more likely that Benedict encouraged his community to read whatever enriched their understanding of the Bible and hastened their steps to God.[19]

5

Benedict Leaves Rome

BENEDICT GAVE UP HIS STUDIES quite suddenly, left Rome, and went in search of solitude in the countryside. According to Gregory, Benedict saw that his classmates were descending into vice and realised that, if he continued to associate with them, he too would be ruined in body and soul (*Dialogue* intro.). Rome offered many vulgar amusements in its streets and many sensual pleasures in its taverns and we can readily believe that Benedict would have shrunk from a life of tight wineskins and loose women. Even so, Gregory makes Benedict's reaction too extreme to be entirely convincing. The nature of life in Rome could not have been entirely unexpected; in any case, Benedict must surely have had ways of avoiding company that he did not wish to keep and of finding more congenial ways of spending his time. Would he really have thrown up his education and dashed his father's hopes for his future career just because of his classmates' behaviour? Gregory does not describe how Benedict reached such a drastic decision, even though he spends many pages of the *Dialogue* describing Benedict's later spiritual development.

Saint Benedict in his Community

It would seem natural for a provincial boy who recoiled from the life of the metropolis to go back to his parents. Instead Benedict went suddenly into a kind of exile at Affile (Effile), a small town 50 kms to the east. Gregory tells us, rather confusingly, that Benedict wished 'to please God alone' and went looking for the monastic habit that would be his entry into a holy life (*Dialogue* intro.). If he had wanted to be alone with God as a hermit, he could have gone straight to the mountains; if he had wanted to become a monk, he could have stayed in Rome, where there were monasteries with a range of ascetic charisms to choose from. Instead he went to Affile, taking with him the 'nurse', or housekeeper, who had been looking after him in Rome. The housekeeper was probably a slave, as domestic servants of that type almost always were, and as a slave she would have been the legal property of Benedict's father and therefore unable to go anywhere without his consent. We may infer from her presence that Benedict had not severed his family links and still had some family backing. These links may have smoothed his path to Affile, since we are also told (*Dialogue* 1.1) that he was welcomed by the 'fine men' who managed the church of St Peter in the town.[1] Clearly these men did not see Benedict simply as a university drop-out; there was something about him that engaged their support. And yet Gregory's account gives the impression that Benedict left Rome without a settled purpose and that it was really at Affile, rather than in Rome, that he decided to turn his back on society and embark on a life of asceticism.

It was at Affile that Benedict performed the first of the miracles recounted in Gregory's *Dialogue*. His housekeeper had borrowed a sieve, but carelessly allowed it to fall off the kitchen table; to her horror, she found that 'the vessel was broken'. Benedict picked up the pieces, prayed over them and the sieve was miraculously restored. Gregory's choice of words would have reminded his readers of the lament in Psalm 31(30):12 — 'I have become like a broken vessel'. It may be that Gregory intended the sieve to be a metaphor for Benedict himself and the verses of the psalm to be a commentary on Benedict's transition in Affile from fear and perplexity to a new confidence in God's protection and the possibility of a life made whole again through prayer.[2]

The time-scale for all these events is uncertain. If Benedict had failed to settle into his Roman lodgings or his course of studies, he probably would have returned fairly quickly to his parents, as unhappy freshmen tend to do. The fact that he went instead to Affile suggests that by that time Benedict was older and more independent. The prose style of the *Rule*, though not of the highest quality, suggests that Benedict stayed long enough in Rome to derive some benefit from his tutors. In Affile he stayed long enough to acquire a reputation as a miracle-worker and then for this to become an embarrassment (*Dialogue* 1.2). We might, therefore, assume that Benedict's time in Rome should be measured in years rather than in months and his time in Affile in weeks rather than in days.

Gregory's account of Benedict's sudden departure from Rome is unconvincing in various ways. There is, it must be said, a suspicion that the story of the dissolute students is no more than a hagiographer's device for glossing over something in his subject's career that was difficult and embarrassing to explain. Was there anything going on in Rome at the time which might have had a sudden impact on a serious young man and made it necessary for him to leave the city quickly? Indeed there was.

6

The Church Divided

THE CHURCH IN ROME was in the grip of a double schism: a conflict with the provinces of the East over theology and strife in Rome itself over rival candidates for the papacy.

The theological conflict was more than a century old. Most Christians now accepted that Christ was both fully human and fully divine. The problem was to know exactly how this was to be understood. Some people in the Church's eastern provinces, particularly in Antioch and Constantinople, emphasised the distinction between the divine and human natures that were 'conjoined' in the person of Jesus, the former being the source of his divine acts and the latter of his human behaviour. This view was particularly associated with Nestorius, a disciple of the leading Antiochene theologians, who became archbishop of Constantinople in 428. Other people, especially in Egypt, were appalled at the thought that there might not be an essential union between the natures in Christ. If that was so, they asked, which nature had been nailed to the Cross? Had the human condition been fully experienced by the Word? Had humanity been fully redeemed?[1]

An alternative Christology had been forcefully articulated by Cyril, the bishop of Alexandria from 412 until his death in 444. Cyril had argued that the Word became flesh as an act of grace, taking upon itself full human life, including a human soul and the capacity to suffer, without ceasing at the same time to be itself. Thus God-in-the-flesh existed in a single subject with God-in-himself. Cyril summed this up in a phrase that epitomised his theology: 'the one incarnate nature of the Word'.[2] Cyril also championed the idea that Jesus's mother should be referred to as *Theotokos* or 'God-bearer' because, when the Word 'came to man in the assumption of flesh and blood even so he remained what he was, that is God in nature and in truth'.[3] Cyril's theology attracted many fervent admirers, who formed the 'one-nature'—or Monophysite—movement within the eastern provinces of the Church. Cyril's use of *Theotokos* tapped into a veneration of the Virgin that was becoming widespread and deeply felt.

An ecumenical Council at Ephesus in 431 was the occasion for a confrontation between Cyril and Nestorius, at which the latter was discredited and sent into exile. With Nestorius out of the way, Cyril was anxious to be reconciled with the other Antiochene theologians and this was achieved by an exchange of letters in 433. Cyril appeared to concede a distinction of natures in Christ, but only if they were within a single person formed by an 'ineffable union' of perfect divinity and perfect humanity.[4] This phraseology allowed many supporters on both sides to go on thinking what they had thought before and the controversy continued.

In 451 the emperor summoned another Council of the Church to meet at Chalcedon, on the outskirts of Constantinople, and produce a definitive statement of belief. The Council was presented with a theological summary by Pope Leo I (the *Tome of Leo*) which the delegates proceeded to take apart, line by line, and test for orthodoxy against the writings of Cyril. The outsome was a compromise. The Chalcedonian definition said that Christ should be acknowledged 'in two natures'—a fateful phrase, which the Monophysites rushed to denounce—while adding many qualifications emphasising the unity of Christ, which were drawn from Cyril's theology.[5] Indeed, the Council said it had accepted Cyril's writings, though it did not specify which ones—and some were more problematic than others. For Rome, the Chalcedonian definition became the new orthodoxy; for many in the East it was a great betrayal. The Monophysites were left unsatisfied and the controversy became a seriously destabilising force in the eastern parts of the empire.

All of this took place before Benedict was born, but he could not have been unfamiliar with the issues because they were hotly debated in Rome while he was a student there. In 482 the Emperor Zeno, far from secure on his throne in Constantinople, decided to look for a formula that would calm the discontent in the East while asserting his imperial role in doctrinal matters to all parts of the empire. With the help of Acacius, the patriarch of Constantinople, he issued an edict known as the *Henotikon*. This avoided contentious phrases from either side of the controversy, but it tilted the debate in a more Monophysite direction and implied that Chalcedon might even be a source of heresy.[6] It caused enormous offence in the West because of the autocratic way that the emperor and the patriarch had presumed to make theology for the whole empire. The current pope (Simplicius, 468–83) was furious, his successors even more so. Pope Gelasius (492–6) reasserted, in the most arrogant tones, the Chalcedonian definition of 'two natures' and denounced anyone who mingled 'in defiled communion' with Acacius.[7] The next pope, Anastasius (496–8), seemed more inclined to compromise. He wrote soothingly to the emperor and declared himself in favour of reconciliation while setting very few preconditions for it. This approach caused alarm among sections of the Italian clergy.

In 498, when Anastasius died, the different attitudes to the *Henotikon* were made manifest in two rival popes, elected within a few hours of each other. One was Symmachus, a Sardinian, a recent convert to Catholicism and one of the city's deacons, who was elected by the hardliners; the other was Laurentius, a priest from Rome itself and the choice of the more pro-eastern party. Laurentius was heavily backed by the senatorial aristocracy as well as a number of senior priests in Rome, but the bulk of the clergy, anxious about the *Henotikon*, backed Symmachus. Theoderic was asked to adjudicate between the two and plumped for Symmachus, since he had been elected first, albeit by only a few hours. A synod of reconciliation followed a few months later, at which Symmachus was confirmed in office and Laurentius agreed to move to a bishopric in Campania.[8] On the issue of the *Henotikon* the new pope returned to the inflexible stance of Gelasius and relations between the papacy and Constantinople remained in deep-freeze for the rest of his pontificate.

That, however, was not the only issue in the disputed election. The pro-eastern party complained that Symmachus was selling off Church property to repay people for their support during his election; that he had celebrated Easter according to the Roman calendar, which differed from the Greek calendar of conventional usage by nearly a month; and that he had been keeping company with disreputable women, in particular a lady named Conditaria ('Spicy'). Theoderic ordered Symmachus to come to Ravenna and explain himself, but during the journey, at an overnight stop in Rimini, Symmachus saw a group of women from the Roman *demi-monde* parading along the beach—a charade that had apparently been arranged by Theoderic himself. Realising that his private life would come under further scrutiny, Symmachus abruptly returned to Rome, where he shut himself up in St Peter's.

Theoderic now appointed a Visitor to run the See of Rome, Bishop Peter of Altinum, and told the Church's bishops to meet and sort things out. These meetings dragged on through much of 502. Symmachus refused to cooperate as long as the Visitor was, in effect, usurping his position as pope, so the synod's enquiry got nowhere, yet Theoderic would not allow the bishops to give up and go home. In the meantime, the pro-eastern faction in the senate brought Laurentius back to the city, where he occupied the papal offices in the Lateran. Supporters of the rival camps fought each other in the streets and much blood was shed. Eventually the members of the synod held up their hands in despair, acknowledged Symmachus as pope and said they would leave his past actions to the judgement of God.

While the synod met ineffectually, Symmachus had been busy: he had ordained more than a dozen new priests to compensate for defections among his supporters and he had spent considerable sums of money on charitable works for the city's poor. When Symmachus himself called a synod at St Peter's in November 502 to celebrate his confirmation in office, it could be seen that most of the priests from churches in Rome were absent, as were many bishops from the dioceses nearby, but their places were filled by younger priests and bishops from remote corners of the country, who were encouraged by noisy support from crowds of ordinary people outside the cathedral. Symmachus took the opportunity to deliver a diatribe against lay interference in the business of the Church, couched in general terms but dealing particularly with the issue of Church property, on which he had reforms to announce. That seems to have been music to the ears of the bishops present, but it sounded a note of warning to priests of the churches in Rome, who had been accustomed to working closely with lay patrons in the management of their buildings and activities. This support in the city's churches enabled Laurentius to stay on in the Lateran. Sporadic disorder continued in the streets until 506, when Theoderic ordered a leading pro-eastern senator to send Laurentius off to retirement on his country estate and ensure that all Roman churches were handed over to Symmachus.[9]

Benedict may have been at one of the higher schools in Rome when the schism broke out. If so, it must be a possibility that he became involved with one of the factions and attracted hostility from people in the other. Since the Laurentians were the losers in the struggle and many of them went into temporary exile, it may be that Benedict was among those forced to leave the city. There is some slight support for this idea in the legend that Benedict's home during his Roman years was in the Trastevere district of the city; if so, he could well have had hostile neighbours, since Trastevere was strongly Symmachan in it sympathies. Gregory does not, of course, mention any of this in his *Dialogue*; the issues were far too complex and he would not have wanted to dwell on the story of a rift at the top of the Church. He would have thought it preferable, therefore, to fall back on the conventions of saintly hagiography and emphasise Benedict's disgust with the lewd behaviour of his classmates.[10]

What is certain is that even if Benedict was not actively involved in the schism—perhaps not even in Rome at the time—he would have known about the events of those years and the issues underlying them. The schism was symptomatic of controversies that reverberated through the Church for the whole of Benedict's lifetime and it is inconceivable that he did not have an opinion about them. Where might his sympathies have lain?

On the Christological issues in general and the *Henotikon* in particular, it seems more likely that Benedict would have preferred the conciliatory approach of Anastasius and the pro-eastern party to the hard-line stance of Gelasius and Symmachus. The dominant tone of the *Rule* is one of reason and moderation. Benedict did not close down theological debate in the monastery; on the contrary, each night, at Vigils, he prescribed readings from 'well-known and approved Catholic Fathers' (*RB* 9.8) to help explain the readings from scripture. He recommended an eclectic approach to theology and the Christian tradition as a whole through a broad study of the Holy Fathers of both East and West (*RB* 73). In particular, he recommended both Basil and Cassian though their writings are, in some respects, not easy to reconcile; it seems that he wanted his monks to hold their differing views together in creative tension. He gave himself the opportunity to shape the monks' beliefs with the commentaries that he gave on the readings at mealtimes (*RB* 38.8–9). It seems that Benedict was content to let theological differences work themselves out in the search for a higher truth. If 'thorns of contention' did appear, he reminded the monks, by a solemn recitation of the Lord's Prayer, that they were a community of prayer and a school of the Lord's service, not a theological seminary (*RB* 13.12).[11]

There is no doubt that Cyril of Alexandria would have been among the 'reputable and orthodox catholic Fathers' that were read in the oratory. Whatever the excesses perpetrated by Cyril's followers after his death and whatever the trouble they were then causing in the East, it was clear that the Council of Chalcedon had endorsed 'the synodical letters of the blessed Cyril' as providing 'an understanding of the saving creed'.[12] Benedict would therefore not have hesitated to read some of Cyril's letters alongside the *Tome of Leo* or the works of other theologians of East or West.

In clarifying his own thoughts on the nature of Christ, Benedict might well have turned to the writings of a theologian he trusted, John Cassian.[13] Benedict's admiration for Cassian's *Conferences* and *Institutes* is clearly displayed in the pages of the *Rule*, so it would have been surprising if he had not also read Cassian's other major work, *On the Incarnation of the Lord against Nestorius*.[14] Cassian wrote this in about 430 as a summary of orthodox belief and a polemic against the two-nature theologians of the time. In his description of the single person of Christ his language comes close to Cyril's, using the terminology of 'flesh' and insisting that 'the Son of Man is the same Person as the Word of God'.[15] Cassian also wrote about the Virgin Mary in terms that Cyril was currently trying to promote. Cassian largely ignored Christ's earthly ministry, apart from the Passion and the Resurrection; Benedict took a similar approach, referring to Christ's teaching but not at all to the events and miracles of Christ's earthly life.

Both Cassian and Cyril were discriminating in the nomenclature that they used in their Christological writings, confining the name 'Jesus' to passages where they were discussing particular aspects of the Word's human manifestation. Cyril laid down a general principle on this point by saying that 'the Only Begotten Word of God himself, as he becomes flesh, is called Christ'.[16] Whether consciously or not, Benedict followed Cyril's example in his studied avoidance of the name 'Jesus' in the *Rule*.

Disputed papal elections were common in late antiquity—there were to be two more of them in Benedict's lifetime—and the electoral process was often scandalously corrupt. In 498 it was far from clear which candidate had been properly elected. Most of the priests who served in the city's churches were dismayed at the outcome. Dionysius Exiguus gave them some backing, though he worked hard for a reconciliation and soon made his peace with Symmachus; so did a deacon John, almost certainly the John who became pope in 523. For most people, however, the factional hostility of the Laurentian schism took years to subside. Symmachus appointed so many priests and deacons—proportionately more

The Church Divided

than all the other popes combined between 492 and 526—that he dictated the character of the Church for the next generation and it was years before some of the Laurentians could be reconciled.

Opposition to Symmachus increased in the months immediately after his election. His alteration of the date of Easter was a reminder of his hostility to things eastern, and it raised an anxiety in some people's minds that if the dates of Easter had been wrong in the past, the baptisms conferred on those days might not be valid. The rumours about Conditaria, if true, were certainly not to the credit of someone who aspired to be head of the ecclesiastical household.[17] Most important by far, however, was the way that Symmachus proposed to handle Church property, a proposal with serious implications for Church life at the local level.

In the early centuries of Christianity, religious observance had been largely a private matter. Most Christian households kept up a rhythm of prayer from dawn to dusk, observed rites like lamp-lighting and venerated relics or shrines of family martyrs. Where possible, special rooms were set aside for worship and in due course a family of modest wealth, as Benedict's was, might incorporate a chapel in the layout of its house. Despite the gradual development of an institutional Church, 'daily domestic prayer continued to be the seedbed of Christian daily life'.[18] On saints' days or major festivals, people flocked to the city's great cathedrals, but their regular Sunday worship usually took place in one of the local churches that had been built in various parts of the city in the decades after 380.

Many of these churches, known as *tituli*, were founded, endowed or handsomely embellished by wealthy lay people. In 499 there were 29 of them. Some of the *tituli* were newly built, but more than half were conversions of the reception halls of aristocratic villas, still with their original columned aisles and apses and sometimes still with mosaics of pagan design. Some of them had now been churches for several generations. Bishops might be partners in *tituli* foundations but powerful lay donors inevitably considered that it was they, and not the bishop, who had the paramount interest in a church which had been identified so closely with their family's status in a particular neighbourhood and often commemorated an ancestor who had been martyred in the days of persecution. The *tituli* had their own liturgies and baptisteries and gradually drew in a congregation from people living round about. Their priests took care of the tombs of local people and administered the communal cemetery. Together with a small band of assistants, both ordained and lay, these priests ran the religious life of the locality in conjunction with the benefactor and important local families, 'almost as self-sufficient microcosms of the Church'.[19]

There is no doubt that popes had a right to sell, reinvest and generally manage property in Rome for the benefit of the Church as a whole; the very term *titulus* was an indication that a particular piece of property had been legally acquired by the Church

The Church Divided

through a donation. But wealthy families wanted their donations to go on being used as originally intended;[20] if changes had to be made, they wanted to do this themselves in conjunction with their local priest, so that their ancestors' memories could be preserved in the customary ways. Symmachus seemed to be threatening these long-established conventions of lay involvement in the running of local churches. In the reforms he announced at the synod in 502, Symmachus conceded that he, as bishop, should not sell urban property belonging to the *tituli*, but he also decreed that their priests should not do so either—a neat way of frustrating his opponents. It was no coincidence that at the start of the schism many priests of the *tituli* backed Laurentius, himself a priest of the *titulus Praxedis*, or that they rallied increasingly to his side, for Laurentius was able to count on the loyalty of most churches in Rome from 502 until his forcible retirement in 506.

These little religious corporations of local clergy and leading families would have been very familiar to Benedict; he would have known them in Nursia during his boyhood and found them in Rome when he went there as a student. A similar group of clergy and elite families may have constituted the 'fine men' who received him at St Peter's in Affile (*Dialogue* 1.1). As the elites of the provincial towns were normally part of a political and social network that reached up to the senatorial aristocrats of Rome, it could well be the case that, if Benedict was a Laurentian sympathiser, his flight to Affile was a move along a network of Laurentian sympathisers. A similar model of cooperation between clergy and local elites may have been in Benedict's mind when he wrote in the *Rule* about the dismissal of an incompetent abbot; in such a case, he said, the diocesan bishop and 'the local abbots or Christians' should take the initiative in replacing him (*RB* 64.4).

The *tituli* of Rome were not just the centre of worshipping communities; they also offered philanthropic support to their members in time of need. They therefore controlled little networks of patronage and dependence through which the elite families of the *tituli* extended an influence over particular neighbourhoods of the city. This could be seen most clearly in the organisation of the city's food supply. For many centuries a large proportion of the population had been fed with rations of wheat, provided free or at subsidised prices from the emperor's vast estates. The rations were not a system of poor relief; they were part of the privilege of being a Roman citizen. The food was given to the middling ranks of society as well as to some — but not all — of the poor. In due course the wheat was replaced with bread and augmented with rations of pork, wine and olive oil.

During the fifth century, the imperial wheat-producing estates of north Africa fell into the hands of the Vandals, while the emperor's attention focused more and more upon the politics of Constantinople. The issue of official rations in Rome did not end, but it was increasingly run by the city's elite, supplied from their estates in Sicily and southern Italy, and

The Church Divided

distributed, in part, through the *tituli*. The latter's philanthropy was more truly charitable than the official ration system had been. Special care was given to widows and orphans—and there were many of them in a city as unhealthy as Rome. Help was also given to members of Christian families who had fallen into poverty, as well as to strangers and people on the margins who had not been registered as Roman citizens and who would previously have been thrown out of the city when food ran short. There was also a change in the way that these recipients of patronage were being perceived. Rather than being 'the people of Rome' they were now being seen as 'the people of God'; those that were on the margins were not 'others' but 'brothers'.[21]

Some charitable relief was now being given by the papal officials to people on the very margins of Roman society; the Vatican Hill, in particular, became known as a place where beggars could go for food. During the fifth century this almsgiving increased in volume and was organised by the city's deacons, using produce from the Church's own landed estates. Symmachus was much identified with this aspect of the Church's work. After his election to the papacy, he immediately set about building new facilities for the poor at St Peter's, with a fountain and public toilets near the atrium of the cathedral and a shelter for the destitute nearby.[22] It was clear that the centrally directed philanthropy of the Church would encroach upon the networks of patronge coming from the *tituli*. This, in turn, would undermine the social influence and political power of the *tituli's* aristocratic patrons.

The same tension between local traditions and central initiatives could be seen in the countryside, where landlords had played a crucial role in spreading Christianity to the rural population, building churches, appointing priests and using their seigniorial influence to convert family members, servants and slaves. The involvement of powerful families in the local life of the Church left bishops with a difficult balance to find: on the one hand, they wanted to encourage aristocratic involvement and charitable endowments, but on the other, they did not want the families to go too far as 'religious impresarios in their own right'.[23] This tension was very evident in Benedict's lifetime as centralising popes like Gelasius and Symmachus tried to control endowments and other religious practices. Gelasius ruled that churches should not be consecrated by the local bishop without papal permission; in practice, however, it seems likely that powerful landowners built a church first and then leant on a bishop to perform the consecration, leaving the pope with little alternative but to endorse what had been done. Popes were more successful in controlling the number of martyr shrines. During the sixth century the names of family martyrs were gradually removed from rural churches, as well as from Roman *tituli*, and replaced with more neutral dedications. The same desire to curb the growth of local centres of spiritual authority lay behind a ban on baptisteries

The Church Divided

in *tituli* and private churches, so that baptisms had to be carried out in a bishop's church and the loyalties of new Christians were focused on the bishop. An important part of local religious leadership was the estate owner's right to appoint his own clergy from someone living on the estate. Early in the sixth century this was confirmed, with the proviso that the local bishop had to approve the appointment, but as late as the 550s the pope was still struggling to get that proviso recognised in every case. Estate clergy were very much under the landlord's thumb and took their orders accordingly, rather than from the bishop.

This was the religious culture in which Benedict was born and grew up. Coming from a background of family piety and lay-clerical cooperation, Benedict may well have thought that Laurentius, with his experience of collaboration with the laity in the *tituli*, would have represented the Roman traditions of prayer and worship more sympathetically than Symmachus, the outsider and hard-line bureaucrat. Benedict would have regarded lay initiative and lay leadership as perfectly natural, as the normal way of getting things done in the Church of those days. We need to see Benedict's monasticism, not just as descending from the earlier forms of monastic life in West and East, but as reflecting the character of Christian life at the local level in central Italy in the late fifth and early sixth centuries.

While the ecclesiastical tensions in Italy were mainly between central direction and local traditions, those in the East continued to be about Christology. In 518 the emperor Justin came to the throne. He was a convinced Chalcedonian and wanted to begin repressive measures against the Monophysites. Before he could do this, he had to bring himself back into accord with Rome. In 519 a delegation from Pope Hormisdas (514–23) arrived in Constantinople and struck a deal with the patriarch and the emperor. It was agreed to anathematise Acacius and everyone associated with the *Henotikon*—even the previous two emperors—and Rome's leadership in the Church was restated. This satisfied Hormisdas, who had always been more concerned with discipline than with dogma. The decisions at Chalcedon were confirmed, but talk of the need for 'accuracy' showed that differences had still not been fully resolved.

Christological controversy now ran right through society in the East. A pro-Chalcedon faction had survived, most prominently in Constantinople, western Syria and in Palestine, which was always more open to ideas from the West because of the constant flow of pilgrims to Jerusalem. Another faction continued to champion the *Henotikon*, seeing it as a potential 'middle way'. On the other hand, many of the Monophysites wanted an explicit rejection of Chalcedon and Leo's *Tome*.[24] These differences were no longer just an esoteric theological debate: bishops were murdered, monks were driven out of their monasteries into the desert, and riots broke out when people from one faction arrived in a city controlled by another. The government had real cause for alarm: if, for example, there was serious disturbance in Alexandria, could the vital grain exports to Constantinople be maintained? If monasteries on the border with Mesopotamia became disaffected, could their loyalty be guaranteed in a war with Persia? There was widespread anxiety in the general population. If a local priest belonged to a 'heretical' faction, would his baptisms be valid? If not, would his parishioners die without benefit of the sacrament? Was all this upheaval a sign that the old gods were coming back to take their revenge?

During the negotiations of 519 between Justin and Hormisdas, an unofficial attempt had been made to bring the Christological factions together. This was based on the belief—now widely accepted in both West and East—that all of Cyril's letters had been endorsed at Chalcedon and it was therefore legitimate to explain the decisions of the Council in terms that were closer to Cyril at his most uncompromising, the position that the Monophysites so admired. This task was attempted by a group of Scythian monks in a document that came to be known as the 'Theopaschite Confession'.[25] The monks stated their belief that Christ was 'in two natures, that is of divinity and humanity, united and unconfused in one person or subsistence', born of the *Theotokos*, and 'essentially or naturally united to the flesh ... not in an empty show of words, not in a small part of himself, but by his Nature', so that in becoming the individual subjective reality of Jesus Christ, he 'suffered no increase or diminution thereby, but remained the full and perfect God the Word'. Having explained Christ in these terms, it became possible to argue more convincingly that, while he remained 'impassible and immortal' as the Word, he also suffered and tasted death in the flesh and did so because 'he made his own the flesh which is capable of death'.[26]

The monks came to Constantinople in 518 and presented their thesis to Justin, who turned it down flat. They then sent a deputation to Hormisdas, who was suspicious and avoided giving an endorsement. Elsewhere in Rome and the West, however, the monks found more support.[27] Their compatriot, Dionysius Exiguus, translated eastern texts to bolster their case and some others who had been associated with the pro-eastern faction in the 490s were sympathetic.

The monks did make one important convert — Justinian. Having been hostile initially, he suddenly realised the political potential of theopaschism. When he came to the throne in 527 he began to move imperial policy in a theopaschite direction, not as an attack on Chalcedon but as a way of emphasising its Cyrilline characteristics and making it more palatable to the Monophysites. This was a compromise that came to be known as neo-Chalcedonianism. Justinian worked hard at this, explaining himself and consulting widely, but the Monophysites — now split into various warring sects — were impossible to unite behind the new formula.

One thing that the Monophysites shared was a hatred of three theologians of the previous century who had been critical of Cyril, either openly or by implication. Justinian decided to add a condemnation of all three to his theological edicts as a way of indicating his distance from the 'two-nature' Christology that Cyril had excoriated. Unfortunately this antagonised many churchmen in the West and blew up into a new controversy known as the Three Chapters. Imperial agents went to Rome, seized the pope, Vigilius (537–55), and escorted him to Constantinople where, in 548, after months of pressure, he caved in and condemned the Chapters. This caused a storm of protest in Western synods and a group of African bishops went so far as to excommunicate him. Justinian next proposed a full ecumenical Council of the Church to approve a neo-Chalcedonian Christology of his own design, combining theopaschite canons with a condemnation of the Three Chapters. Vigilius then reverted to his original stance and refused to agree. Months of humiliation followed, in which Vigilius was put under house arrest and manhandled by Justinian's soldiers. When the Council opened in May 553, he at first refused to attend, but in December he gave up and grudgingly accepted Justinian's proposals. Once again, there was a furious reaction in the West and the province of Aquileia (in north-eastern Italy) declared itself to be out of communion with Rome. In the East, the splintered factions of the Church remained unreconciled.

The dogmatic canons of the Council of Constantinople had little impact in the West; they were, in any case, not so much a revision of dogma as a clarification of ideas that were already inherent in the

Definition of Chalcedon.[28] The Three Chapters, on the other hand, aroused furious and widespread dissent, at a popular level as well as among the clergy. What was at issue here was the new form of centralised Church which Justinian seemed to be imposing, a Church based in Constantinople and directed by the emperor. Instead, Christians in Italy wanted to maintain their traditional ecclesial model, dating back to the earliest times, a model of 'churches united behind their bishops and made one by communion'.[29]

Benedict may have died before the storm really broke over the Three Chapters; even so, he and his community lived through a period of extraordinary instability in Church governance and doctrine. To pass through all this turbulence, the monks remained 'discerning and moderate', as their abbot was (*RB* 64.17), focused always on their life of prayer, based on the psalms. This was their point of entry into a more profound stability, a stability greater than anything then offered by Church doctrine—a stability of heart and mind in the service of Christ.

7

The Monastery in the World

AFTER A SHORT TIME IN AFFILE, Benedict walked into the hills near Subiaco and found shelter in a cave deep in the forest. His first years in this cave undoubtedly contained long periods of solitude, physical hardship and prayerful contemplation of God. Gradually, however, the world outside began to impinge upon him.

His firsr visitor was Romanus, a monk from a nearby monastery (*Dialogue* 1.4–5). The two men met when Benedict first arrived in the area and Romanus kept in touch, visiting Benedict's cave from time to time and bringing pieces of bread and, on one occasion, a monk's habit for him to wear. Romanus was probably foraging for his fellow monks, looking for things like chestnuts and wild honey which monasteries commonly used to supplement their diet. Perhaps he gave Benedict advice on how to forage for his own diet. No doubt the two of them also talked about God and compared the life of hermits with that of monks in community.

The next visitor was a priest who brought Benedict an Easter meal, tipped off, perhaps, by Romanus. Then Benedict was discovered by shepherds. Inevitably, it was not long before the local villagers began to hear about the holy man in the Subiaco cave. Benedict would have found himself in the relationship that often developed between Christian solitaries and the population round about them. Many of the country people, if they were Christians at all, were Christians in name only; they would have consulted pagan soothsayers rather than the local priest and held ceremonies at sacred trees and springs more often than they went to church. Benedict would have offered them a Christian solution to the difficulties of their lives; he would have encouraged them to pray and given them spiritual nourishment in exchange for the food which they brought to him (*Dialogue* 1.8). The impact on Benedict himself must have been profound. His privileged upbringing was little material use to him here; now he was a man with nothing, listening carefully to people who had very little. He would have come to understand their anxieties about weather and crops, their concerns about the health of their animals and their families, their conflicts with difficult neighbours and their fear of demons and extraordinary natural events. Much of what he heard would not have been trivial or irrational; indeed, he probably came to respect the folk wisdom of the country people. This contributed to his open-mindedness and his ability, as shown in the *Dialogue*, to engage with people from many different backgrounds.

Gradually Benedict's reputation for wisdom and holiness began to spread and people came to join him in the forest (*Dialogue* 2.3). His reputation attracted the attention of monks at Vicovaro, a place not far from Subiaco. Their abbot had recently died and they invited Benedict to replace him. Unfortunately, Benedict found the community to be both undisciplined and unwilling to reform and after a period of acute tension, he withdrew and returned to his solitude in the forest.[1]

Back again in Subiaco, Benedict began to attract the support of wealthy patrons. Young men of noble families were sent to join him and donations would certainly have been made to support the fledgling community (*Dialogue* 3.13–14). Settling the monks under a rule of life was now a necessity. It is possible that Benedict was already reading Cassian's *Conferences* for guidance to the solitary life, so that when followers gathered about him his focus shifted to Cassian's writings about communal living. Benedict may also have read Athansius's *Life of Antony*, since Antony's spiritual quest had been so similar to his own. From there, his thoughts may have moved on to the Desert Fathers and their reflections on solitude and on life in community. Benedict always held Cassian and the Desert Fathers in particularly high regard (*RB* 73.5). For guidance in practical matters Benedict leant upon the various short rules that had been written in Gaul and Italy in the late fifth and early sixth centuries, rules that emerged when abbots had consulted together about common problems.[2] The influence of these sources can be seen in parts of Benedict's own *Rule*, such as the chapters dealing with discipline and the reception of guests and postulants.

When Benedict came to write his own *Rule* he borrowed extensively from the *Rule of the Master*. This had been written by an anonymous Italian abbot, probably in the first quarter of the sixth century and probably in the area south-east of Rome. Benedict and the Master were therefore contemporaries.[3] However, it would be wrong to assume that Benedict followed the Master from the start. There is no evidence that the Master's *Rule* was in circulation — or even written — when the Subiaco community was beginning to form. In any case, the Master's *Rule* may not have appealed to Benedict at first; he probably still hoped to resume his solitary life and would have been reluctant to accept the abbatical role that was being thrust upon him. Benedict may also have been put off by the Master's tendency to ramble and his lack of moderation. Rather than adopting the *Rule of the Master* for his young community, it is more likely that Benedict went through a long period of experiment, lasting perhaps twenty years, when he drew upon the same written sources that the Master had used, tried out ideas of his own, consulted with his monks and sometimes changed course. When Benedict eventually sat down to write his own *Rule*, the convergence between his text and the Master's is not surprising, since both authors came from the same cultural background, faced the same problems, and worked in the same religious and social context.

The Monastery in the World

Legend has it that the young community took up residence in the ruins of a villa built near Subiaco for the emperor Nero, which looked out across an artificial lake created by a dam across the River Anio.[4] The villa contained a reception hall which would have been ideal as a church, but there is no surviving evidence of the structure being altered to accommodate a community of monks. Perhaps the community did not stay there long; the villa was next to a road and the monks would have found it difficult to get the privacy they needed. The rest of the flat land in the neighbourhood was probably occupied by farmers from Subiaco, and the monks would have had to retreat to the hillsides. These are exceptionally steep and the monastic buildings had to perch on ridges or cling to ledges. The monks found themselves divided into twelve priories, each a mile or two from the next and each containing about a dozen monks. It was a very inconvenient layout for a community that was supposed to be united and enclosed.

A second problem was water supply. On one occasion a deputation of monks from three of the priories came to Benedict to complain about the dangers they faced when picking their way down the hillside to collect river water. 'The priories will have to be moved to other sites', they concluded (*Dialogue* 5.1). Benedict surveyed the hillside and told them to dig next morning at a place where he had left a small pile of stones. Abundant water was uncovered. This would not have solved the problem for the community as a whole. In this part of central Italy, where a gap of two or three months between significant rainfalls is normal, every monastery needed either easy access to a perennial source—a river, a spring, or a plentiful well—or else a system for carrying rainwater from its roof to a cistern of adequate size. In Monte Cassino this problem was solved by having a large cistern under the oratory, with a small well to draw off the water as required. In recent times there has also been a freshwater spring in the saddle between Monte Cassino and the adjoining Monte Cairo and it may be that this was also available to Benedict's community.[5]

A third problem was to settle the community on an economic foundation that would support it from year to year and continue into the future. While a small community might have lived from hand to mouth on cash donations, a larger one needed a steady and reliable stream of income from land and other investments or from the product of the monks' own labour. Market gardening was almost impossible on those precipitous slopes at Subiaco; self-sufficiency in food was a dream.[6] The monks must have had to buy their supplies in local markets. How did they pay for them? Did they work at simple handicrafts, making things like rush mats and baskets as the Desert Fathers had done before them, and then sell or barter these items in Subiaco or Tivoli? The demand for these products may have been limited and the profits inadequate, particularly as the community increased in size, perhaps to more than 100 brothers. It is safe to assume that wealthy benefactors endowed the monastery in various ways and especially with land, but this did not solve the problem of providing daily work for the monks and a steady income in cash.

What actually precipitated the move away from Subiaco, according to Gregory's account (*Dialogue* 8.1–5), was the deterioration in relations between Benedict and Florentius, the local priest. This was due, says Gregory, to Florentius's envy of Benedict's reputation and the crowds of people who flocked to see him. So bitter did Florentius become that he sent Benedict some poisoned bread, and then, when Benedict saw through this plot, he sent naked girls to dance in the monastery gardens and undermine the brothers' resolve. At this point, according to Gregory, Benedict decided to leave and take a few of his monks to start a new community at Monte Cassino.

It is easy to believe that Benedict had more charisma than the local priest and that the latter's plot was motivated mainly by personal jealousy. There may have been financial competition as well. If this was a time of parish development and church building—as it was—Florentius may have had a half-built church on his hands. Perhaps, like parish priests throughout the ages, he needed money for the roof. To his dismay, donations were flowing instead to the monastery. Florentius may also have begun to meddle in the monastery's affairs. The monks would have been dependent on him to supply consecrated bread for their communion services and Florentius may have seen this as an opportunity to interfere more generally in the life of the community—hence the *Dialogue's* story of the 'blessed bread', the reserved sacrament, with the poison as a metaphor for the conditions that Florentius was trying to attach to it (*Dialogue* 8.2).[7]

The story about the naked dancers need not be taken literally.[8] It may be another metaphor for the way that Florentius was undermining the discipline of the community. It is also an example of the way that Gregory avoided matters of fact and substituted a story from which moral lessons could be drawn. The fact is that Subiaco, always an inconvenient site, had now become seriously impractical. Benedict had gone less than ten miles towards Monte Cassino, so Gregory says (*Dialogue* 8.7), when he heard that Florentius had been killed in an accident, yet he did not turn back. The problem was not so much Florentius as Subiaco.

Benedict would not have uprooted his monks without being sure that their new home would be an improvement on the old—specifically, that they would have a secluded site where they could live together as one community, with agricultural land for their support. Monte Cassino would not have been unclaimed land with no clear owner; it was far too important a place for that. Around the summit was a perimeter wall, within this there were the remains of a Roman fort with walls and towers, still of strategic significance, and at the very summit of the mountain were sites of pagan worship. Benedict

The Monastery in the World

seems to have taken title to the mountain by a normal process of gift or purchase.[9]

For a monastic community, Monte Cassino was a very desirable location, far enough above the world to deter visitors who were merely curious, yet connected to the world in ways useful to the community. To the south and north were hills and forests; to the north-west the Via Latina ran past the town of Aquinum (Aquino) and on to Rome through a tired countryside of grass and scrub, used mainly for grazing; and at the foot of the mountain and stretching to the south-east was the rich plain of Campania, a patchwork of wheat fields, vineyards and vegetable gardens. The Via Latina ran on southwards through Campania to the Bay of Naples and beyond, and it was the main route taken by wealthy people travelling from Rome to their villas around the Bay. Just below the mountain was the town of Casinum (Cassino) with its Roman fort and amphitheatre and its markets and hostelries, which offered a good outlet for the products of the monastic workshops and gardens. The monks could now achieve the economic security that had eluded them in Subiaco.

At Monte Cassino the community seems to have grown very quickly. Before long it was necessary for Benedict to establish a third monastery, this time on donated land at Terracina (Tarracina), near the north-west corner of the Bay of Naples (*Dialogue* 22.1–3). A monastery was built there according to a plan drawn up by Benedict, under an abbot and prior whom he appointed. Terracina was an old fortified town at the southern end of the Appian Way, the alternative route from Rome to the Bay. From the community's point of view it had advantages similar to Monte Cassino's: productive land nearby—in this case including vineyards on the slopes behind the town—and a good flow of customers passing through its markets.

It was probably at this point that Benedict decided to write his *Rule*. He was still abbot of the remaining monks at Subiaco, but his authority now had to be exercised from afar; he had moral authority over the new community at Terracina; and his advancing years must have made him anxious to leave a written legacy for the monks at Monte Cassino.[10] Each of these communities would have benefited from a written guide to the monastic life. This was therefore the moment when the Master's comprehensive overview of monasticism would have been most appealing as a model. At the same time, if Benedict's abbacy was becoming more remote from his communities, he needed to supplement the Master's autocratic attitude to his monks with a more Augustinian emphasis on charitable and supportive relationships between each monk and his fellows. His communities would then have a better chance of survival because they would be bound by mutual love, not just by common obedience to their superior.

Another prompt in putting pen to parchment was Benedict's new neighbour Eugippius, the abbot of a monastery at Castellum Lucullanum, near Naples. Lucullanum was a focal point for a network of monasteries in Campania, thanks to its scriptorium, which copied books that passed up and down the network. Eugippius had patrons among the aristocracy of Rome and the Bay of Naples and a wide circle of correspondents—people like Dionysius Exiguus and Boethius, members of the old Laurentian faction and people with leanings towards the theology of the East. Benedict would certainly have heard about him from his contacts in other monasteries. It is quite possible that they met, since Lucullanum was a relatively short journey along the Via Latina from Monte Cassino.

Eugippius was already known as the compiler of the most elaborate florilegium of Augustine's writings, the *Excerpta Augustini*. Towards the end of his life—and about the time that Benedict moved to Monte Cassino—Eugippius wrote a monastic *Rule*. He began by reproducing two of Augustine's rules in their entirety and then continued with lengthy quotes from the Master, Cassian and Basil, and short extracts from Pachomius and Jerome—a florilegium of monastic writings rather than an exposition of his own views. However, it made the point that the dependence on a powerful abbot, which had been emphasised by Cassian and the Master, should be softened by Augustine's injunction to the monks to live 'in harmony and concord [and] honour God mutually in each other'.[11]

Did the *Rule of Eugippius* encourage Benedict to write a *Rule* of his own? That is quite possible. Did Eugippius introduce Benedict to the *Rule of the*

Master? It is significant that Eugippius did not edit the authors that he quoted except in the case of the Master, and here his alterations are the same as those made by Benedict when quoting the same passages. One possible conclusion is that Benedict copied these from Eugippius and then went on to look at the rest of the Master's text and make further borrowings.[12] It is also possible that Benedict set out either to compile a florilegium of his own, or to make an edition of the Master's *Rule*; either of these projects would have been within the literary conventions of the time. Having embarked on one of these tasks, Benedict realised that the Master's text required so much amendment that it would become an original work of his own; and having seen the juxtaposition of Augustine and Cassian in Eugippius's *Rule*, Benedict realised that a convincing synthesis of the two would be a necessary part of anything he wrote.

Benedict was very free with the Master's text. He made alterations, large and small, he made long deletions and he added passages that were entirely his own. If, in some places, he followed the Master exactly, it must have been because he thought that his own beliefs, refined by many years of experience, were accurately expressed by the Master's words. If he had wanted to change any of these, he would have changed them. So whatever the antecedents of Benedict's text, it is Benedict who speaks to us now.

The move to Monte Cassino had important consequences for the economy of the community and its daily routine. It made it possible, at last, for the monks to supply much of their own food. Self-sufficiency was the ideal: 'then truly are they monks', wrote Benedict, 'if they live by the work of their hands' (*RB* 48.8). They were to exemplify a long-standing belief in Roman society that a garden was the foundation of independence and that a vegetable diet was an honourable one, no matter if it was simple and common. An area of gently sloping land at the top of Monte Cassino could have been used as a vegetable garden and some varieties of herbs might have been grown among the rocks on the flanks of the mountain. A verse in the *Rule* (*RB* 48.7) warns the monks that they might sometimes have to do harvesting themselves, a hint that the monastery owned grain-producing land down on the plain. This is confirmed by another verse (*RB* 50.1) which refers to brothers who work 'at a considerable distance, and who cannot reach the oratory at the right time'. Benedict evidently shared in this work himself, since one of the episodes in the *Dialogue* (32.1–2) tells of a peasant who came to the monastery carrying his dead son, only to find that Benedict was away in the fields.

After a day's work on the plain an ascent of the mountain to eat and sleep in the monastery would have been a challenging prospect, even for the hardiest of monks, so it is likely that the community had an over-night shelter at the mountain's foot, perhaps something like a barn, with space for tools, rudimentary cooking facilities and clean straw for bedding. This may have been the building not far from the monastery gate, which Gregory mentions in the *Dialogue* (33.2). In later centuries this developed into a fully fledged monastery, a twin of the one on the hill, which acted as an office for tenants to pay their rents and a bulking-point where crops could be gathered in and offered to dealers.[13]

Some of the monastery's farms were much further away, perhaps in another province. This would explain the miracle of the bushels of grain described in the *Dialogue* (21.1–2). There had been a poor harvest in Campania and the monks, like the population around them, were down to their last loaves. 'Don't worry', said Benedict, 'tomorrow you'll have all you want'; and the next morning there were bags of grain piled at the monastery's door—obviously the delivery of the harvest from one of the monastery's remoter properties, which Benedict had been expecting.

Through the community's involvement in farming and landowning Benedict must have been brought into contact with the land management system of the time. For many centuries, the most fertile tracts of the countryside had been divided into great estates. Some of these were of astonishing size and complexity: they might total several thousand square miles, be divided into many separate parcels of land and contain a dozen or more villas. The owners of estates such as these could donate a farm to a church or a monastery and hardly notice the difference. The life of an estate revolved around the villa. The great landowners—senators and other members of the elite—saw the villa as a rural retreat where they could retire each year for a month or two of *otium*, or purposeful leisure; here they could spend time reading, ruminating, conversing with friends or admiring their flocks and fruit trees. But in a range of buildings behind the villa—and active all the year round—were hay-lofts, wineries, oil presses, store rooms, pens for animals, quarters for the farm supervisers and barracks for the slaves. A country villa was both an opulent residence and the centre of an agricultural business.

By Benedict's time many of the big estates in central Italy had been subdivided into estates of medium size owned by lawyers, bishops and other well-to-do townspeople, and much of the slave labour had been replaced by rent-paying tenants. In one sense, however, things remained the same: the owners were absentees and the daily management of the estate was in the hands of supervisers. There was a landlord's agent, a *procurator*, who travelled round the parts of a dispersed estate; a *dispensator*, a treasurer or bursar, responsible for handling money and maintaining the inventory of equipment; and a *vilicus*, a steward or farm manager, an experienced agriculturist, who supervised work in the fields. These last two were normally slaves, their loyalty encouraged by the prospect of gaining freedom. When a farm was transferred, it was common for the various functionaries to come with the land in order to ensure continuity. So Benedict, as the new landlord of properties around Monte Cassino, would have found himself at the top of a little pyramid of rural relationships.

Saint Benedict in his Community

Benedict would have dealt most often with a *vilicus*. That man needed to be proficient in the various aspects of agriculture and also be sufficiently literate to keep simple accounts and read veterinary prescriptions. But many of his qualities were those of leadership and moral character. He had to lead his men into the fields, demonstrate how jobs should be done, encourage those who flagged in their work and, at the end of a day, gather them up 'like a good shepherd'. Back in the villa he had to show care to everyone, attend to anyone injured, see that food and clothing were adequate and join the workers in their meal, giving 'an example to them of frugality'. He was to be neither too severe nor too lenient and show such moderation that his firmness was respected. In practice, *vilici* sometimes fell short of the ideal—there are records of oxen being hired out for personal profit or of seed being bought that was never sown—but it is also clear that many of them served their masters well and deserved the honour and wealth that were often bestowed on them.[14]

The language of farm management found its way into the text of the *Rule*. When Benedict wrote about the replacement of an abbot in an emergency, he said that outside authorities should 'set a worthy steward [*dispensator*] over the household of God' (*RB* 64.5) and he went on (64.7) to emphasise that the abbot would have to render to God 'an account of his stewardship', using a quotation from Lk 16:2 and the word *vilicatio*. The general welfare of an estate had always been recognised as the responsibility of the household head, the *dominus*, but in Benedict's scenario—where the abbot is *vilicus* to God's *dominus*—the abbot also has to attend to details and understand the practical aspects of the tasks being carried out by subordinates. The use of the term *dispensator* showed that Benedict also expected an abbot to have financial acumen and an ability to manage the monastery's connections with the affairs of the world.

Benedict's *vilicus* probably lived on the community's home farm at the foot of the mountain, together with a small squad of labourers, some of whom may have been slaves. He would also have employed local tenant families who were tied to the estate and obliged to pay rents in kind or in labour services. The *vilicus* would have needed to organise all this labour effectively, combining it with the work of the monks themselves. No doubt the most physically demanding jobs were done by the tenants and slaves, whereas the monks' contributions were lighter repetitive work such as hoeing weeds, tending vines and gathering in the crops. The monastery farm may also have had a flock of sheep, with a separate squad of shepherds to look after them.[15]

Benedict would have met his *vilicus* at regular intervals. As a good landlord he would also have been expected to make occasional inspections of his properties—it was a maxim of Roman agriculture that 'the best fertiliser is the master's eye'.[16] Benedict would have come to know something of the problems of the countryside; for example, his understanding of the tensions between landlords and tenants may have helped him to reconcile the differences between an impoverished peasant and the landlord Zalla (*Dialogue* 31.1–3).

Many decisions of a practical nature would have been needed to keep the community's estates productive. A steady output of a variety of crops was essential if the community was to be provided with grain, fruit and vegetables and the other agricultural products like olive-oil, wine, sheep's cheese, honey and straw which were needed for comfort and a healthy life.. Some of these products would have been delivered to the monastery's kitchen and cellar, the rest would have gone to the markets of Casinum to be sold for cash.

Unfortunately, these were difficult years for agriculture. Production was disrupted by Justinian's invasion. Demand for produce from Campania would have shrunk as the market in Rome contracted with the city's declining population during the war. Benedict's warning to the monks about having to do the harvesting themselves (*RB* 48.7) is evidence that some of the monastic lands were normally worked by hired labour and this could suddenly run short, as peasants fled from passing armies or succumbed to plague. To make matters worse, for almost the whole of the year 536, and intermittently for some years after, the sky was darkened with a veil of dust which caused a world-wide disruption of normal weather. The sun in Italy shone feebly and cast no shadows, farmers experienced 'a winter without storms, spring without mildness, summer without heat' and their crops withered in 'perpetual frost and unnatural drought'.[17] It must have been extraordinarily difficult to decide what crops to grow and how to ensure a reliable food supply for the monastery. There must have been times when only Benedict's faith persuaded him that another harvest could be gathered in and his community could escape starvation.

The older monks, and those with an aptitude for a particular craft, spent their working hours in the monastic workshop. It is clear that some of the monks were producing goods of high quality (*RB* 57.2), destined for a fashionable clientele in the markets of Casinum. But Benedict warns against any pride in craftsmanship for its own sake or any spirit of commercialism; the artisans were to work humbly, avoid avarice and fraud in their dealings with the secular world and set prices which allowed local craftsmen to take a major share of the market.[18] The monastic workshop recently excavated at the Crypta Balbi in Rome was, in Benedict's lifetime, producing a range of goods in metal, bone and glass to cater both for pilgrims and for the more expensive tastes of the city's elite. There may have been a similar output at Monte Cassino. In particular, some of the monks may have been busy with the production of perfumes. The basic ingredient of perfume was green olive oil and this part of Campania was a major producer of it; the collection of green windfall olives, the start of the process, would have been a suitable form of

Saint Benedict in his Community

light labour for the frail members of the community. Perfumes were made by mashing flowers into the oil, followed by boiling, stirring and straining. Campania produced flowers in abundance and a well-established commercial network, which took in the markets of Casinum and Aquinum, could have kept the monastery supplied with fresh blooms.[19]

The porter, housed at the monastery gate, was a pivotal figure in the community's economic relations with the outside world. It is easy to see why Benedict attached so much importance to his appointment. He needed to be a 'wise old man' (*RB* 66.1), unfailingly courteous but a shrewd judge of character. He had to receive everyone as if they were Christ; yet, at the same time, he had to turn away hucksters and false monks while responding to pilgrims, refugees and the poor people of the locality 'with gentleness and love' (*RB* 66.4). He needed to understand the whole business of the monastery, know which monks needed to receive visitors or messages, judge which dealers and middlemen to admit and which to exclude, and know how all this could be done without disrupting the quiet rhythm of the monks' daily lives. This was no job for a novice.

The porter's was the face that the community presented to individual visitors. At the same time, the monastery was now a local landmark, a prominent landholder and a significant player in the local economy. Benedict had to recognise that his responsibilities extended beyond the monks in his care; he now had to act as a steward—a worthy *dispensator*—

towards society more generally. In the thirty years that he had been attracting followers, Benedict had raised an extraordinary amount of money—enough to build three monasteries and support the lifestyle of perhaps 150 monks, in all[20]—and he would have been thought extremely remiss if he had used this wealth for the community alone without a wider sense of social responsibility.

Over the previous century, Church leaders had persuaded wealthy householders that the bountiful gifts of God's earth should be held in trust for the people of Christ—firstly, that is, for the people of Christ's Church, but then for everyone with whom Christ shared humanity, for people on the margins as well as for impoverished citizens of all classes and backgrounds. Wealth in itself was not to be condemned. If the rich landowner saw himself as a *dispensator* on God's behalf, managing his superfluous wealth with compassion and generosity for the people of God's world, the poor would reciprocate with respect for the rich and the unity of society would be preserved.[21]

This last point was a sensitive one for all ascetic communities with landed wealth and an aristocratic complexion. In the early sixth century, landowners were often critical if one of their number withdrew from the world into an enclosed community and apparently neglected the social leadership that was properly his. It is clear, however, from the stories recorded in the pages of Gregory's *Dialogue*, that Benedict and his monks often reached outside their monastic enclosure to give help and guidance to their neighbours in need. The evidence shows that the community used its material resources for the benefit of people round about by feeding the country folk of Campania in times of famine (*Dialogue* 28.1), sharing the market for handicrafts with local artisans (*RB* 57.8), giving hospitality to visitors (*RB* 53) and receiving the poor 'as Christ' (*RB* 53.15 and 66.3–4).[22]

It is in this context that we should read some of Benedict's instructions to monks about their personal behaviour (*RB* 4). While most of these applied to the community as a whole inside the monastery walls, some of them seem more relevant to the monks' interactions with the surrounding population. For example, a monk travelling through the war-torn districts of Campania in the late 530s might well have felt a responsibility for burying the dead and consoling the sorrowing (*RB* 4.17–19) A monk who went out to do business for the community needed to be free from deceit and be careful to avoid giving 'the kiss of peace insincerely' (*RB* 4.24–5). Monks who worked in the fields and stayed overnight in the shelter at the foot of the mountain presumably rubbed shoulders occasionally with local people and might need to be reminded to refrain from empty chatter and bawdy jokes (*RB* 4.53–4).

Part of the community's role in local society revolved around Benedict personally. His reputation for holiness had followed him from Subiaco and local people began to bring their problems to him for a solution. Even so, Benedict was unwilling to become a celebrity. When a peasant came to the monastery bearing the lifeless body of his son, Benedict was reluctant to try to revive him; he was, he said, unworthy to be compared with the apostles in such a matter (*Dialogue* 32.2) and it was only because of the father's anguish that he was persuaded to make the attempt. He cured a slave of elephantiasis (*Dialogue* 26.1), treated a man with a leprous skin-rash (*Dialogue* 27.3), and gave psychotherapy to a mentally disturbed priest from the diocese of Aquinum (*Dialogue* 16.1). He gave sound advice on practical matters, as when he reconciled the landlord Zalla with his tenant and sorted out the financial problems of a local Christian (*Dialogue* 27.1–2). He could also help with delicate inter- personal relationships, as in the case of two abusive nuns and the victims of their domestic violence (*Dialogue* 23.2–5). In several of the episodes described in the *Dialogue* he exposed deceit in dealings between the monastery and the outside world, as in the case of the monk who hid napkins (*Dialogue* 19.1–2) or the carter Exhilaratus, who hid a keg of wine that was destined for the community (*Dialogue* 18.1). Benedict's dealings with local people were completely evenhanded. The first person he cured was a slave. Of the two people he brought back from the brink of death, one was the son of a peasant and the other the son of a member of the local elite.[23]

Benedict's holiness was so profound that he could often deal with these problems without special divine intervention—a word, a glance or a touch was sufficient. In many cases he relied on prayer—often immediately and publicly, at the moment when the problem was brought to his attention and in the midst of whatever he happened to be doing at the time. On two occasions he found it necessary to use portions of the eucharistic Host, but this was to calm restless spirits who were beyond his reach and beyond the grave.

One of the functions of the holy man in late antique society was to spread the value system of Christianity into peripheral areas of Europe.[24] Campania was hardly peripheral in a geographical sense, but Christianity was peripheral to the lives of many of the inhabitants. In spite of a veneer of Christianity, they continued to acknowledge places of pagan significance—such as springs, trees and hilltops—and evil spirits were still considered to be responsible for crop failure and natural disasters. When Benedict arrived at Monte Cassino there was a grove of trees on the summit of the mountain, a place for the worship of demons (*Dialogue* 8.10), as well as an altar dedicated to the god Apollo.[25] Benedict cut down the trees and replaced the altar with one dedicated to Saint John the Baptist, whose anniversary (24 June) was on Midsummer Day and close to the feast of Apollo at the summer solstice, so that local people who made their annual pilgrimage to the summit for pagan ceremonies found themselves involved in a Christian ceremony instead (*Dialogue* 8.10–11). In this, Benedict was acting both as a holy man and as a good landlord, bringing a deeper knowledge of

The Monastery in the World

Christian values to the locality, providing a place of worship on his estate and leading by example.

Benedict's initiatives did not go uncontested. According to the *Dialogue* 'the devil' tried hard to hamper the construction of the monastery and harm individual monks—as, for example, when he toppled a wall and crushed a monk underneath it (*Dialogue* 11.1). It may be that Gregory intended 'the devil' of the *Dialogue* to be a composite figure representing everything opposed to Christianity, including the various demons, malign spirits and pagan rituals that still haunted the countryside. Benedict's destruction of the trees at the summit of the mountain was an open challenge that the old religious forces could not ignore. 'The devil' remained a thorn in the side of the community until a final showdown took place, also at the summit of the mountain. On that occasion 'the devil' posed as a veterinarian (*Dialogue* 30.1), a personification of the peasants' anxiety over animal health and their dependence on village medicines—two areas of rural life where paganism and magic clung on most tenaciously. In the *Dialogue* Benedict dismissed him with a slap; in real life, he probably just shrugged off the final criticism from the local sorcerer. Benedict and the community had won acceptance from local people, but the process had been a gradual one.[26]

Benedict is said to have made many converts by his constant preaching (*Dialogue* 8.11). It is likely that he spoke to mixed gatherings of people in annual ceremonies at the summit of the mountain. At the same time it is difficult to see how he could have preached regularly to local congregations while observing the terms of his own *Rule*.[27] The *Dialogue* provides no evidence that Benedict planted the Church's liturgy in the locality. The Mass is mentioned only incidentally and priests appear only three times in the *Dialogue's* various episodes, on two occasions in an unfavourable light.[28] What the *Dialogue* really shows is that Benedict taught by example. He demonstrated a loving concern for all his neighbours combined with a prayerful communion with God. He reached out to society while reaching up to God.[29]

Benedict was concerned that his community should have an evenhanded and charitable relationship with the whole of the society around it, from aristocratic patrons to destitute peasants and slaves. Society in Italy was obsessed with status. The ultimate prize for social climbers was membership of the senate, that ancient assembly of 'the best people' in the empire. By the middle of the fifth century many thousands of families had claimed senatorial rank. A new system of grading was imposed on them so that only those of real distinction, the so-called *gloriosi*, actually sat in the senate itself, which returned to its former size as an elite body of office holders and landlords. Some of the members belonged to old landed families like the Anicii and the Decii, celebrated through many generations, but some were men with modest pedigrees and smaller estates who had risen to high office through a combination of education, personal charm, a fortunate marriage and influential connec-

The Monastery in the World

tions. Money was always a crucial element in status. Benedict did not have to tell his monks to be polite to the wealthy 'for the awe felt for the wealthy imposes respect enough of itself' (*RB* 53.15).

The influx into senatorial ranks had originally been led by the equestrians, once an elite cavalry unit in the Roman army but now another landowning class and administrative elite. Their upper grades, such as the *eminentissimi*, merged with the senators, while their lowest grades sank into obscurity. Other ambitious newcomers to the nobility were members of the *curiales*, the provincial aristocracy, who sat on the town councils around the empire and managed public life in their localities, as Benedict's family did in Nursia. These families were eager to rise to a social rank that put them on equal terms with imperial officials and freed them from the burdensome details of local government. Traces of these social distinctions could be found in the monastery. One evening Benedict was eating alone and a young monk, who had come from an equestrian family, was asked to hold a lamp for him. 'Who is this that I'm serving like a slave?', the monk said to himself; but Benedict sensed his hostility and rebuked him (*Dialogue* 20.1–2). It is clear, therefore, that Benedict's family ranked below the equestrians in status but, because of its concern for Benedict's education, it was unlikely to have been below the *curiales* in wealth and aspiration.[30] Other monks also came from the elites. For example, Placid, the young monk who nearly drowned at Subiaco, was the son of a patrician, one of the very highest of the senatorial grades, and another monk who was badly injured during building operations at Cassino was from a family in the *curiales* (*Dialogue* 11.1–2).

Below the elite were the freeborn commoners, the vast majority of the population, ranging from those in respectable professions such as teaching and law to those considered less respectable, such as traders and craftsmen. A significant minority of the total population were freedmen, ex-slaves who had been granted freedom by their masters. Although these people never threw off the stigma of their former condition, it was often the case that, using the knowledge they had gained from carrying on the master's business and using any patronage which he was willing to offer, they were able to leap-frog the ranks of society above them and gain positions of wealth and power. Near the broad base of the social pyramid were the peasantry of the countryside, often miserably poor and suffering from forms of bondage that amounted almost to slavery. Below them were the actual slaves, perhaps 15% of the Italian population. Anyone from these categories of people might ask to join the community and slaves certainly did so (*RB* 2.18).

The formation of slaves into monks was always a delicate matter. Abbots could not allow their monasteries to be seen as bolt-holes for slaves seeking refuge from an angry master or trying to escape from the system as a whole. The Council of Chalcedon ruled that a slave could become a monk only if his master gave permission. A later law said that if the slave subsequently left the monastery, he would revert to his former status. By the middle of the sixth century, perhaps as a result of the social disruption caused by war and epidemics, slaves seem to have been appearing willy-nilly at monastery gates, asking for a postulancy. A law of Justinian laid down how this situation should be handled. Everyone, slave or free, should be admitted for a three-year postulancy, during which they would be counselled by the abbot and their sense of vocation tested. During this time, a master could, if he wished, try to prove that a postulant was a slave, that he had committed a crime and that he had come to the monastery to escape. If the master succeeded, he would be allowed to take the slave away, though he had to pledge not to harm him. Otherwise the slave could remain in the monastery, 'freed from the insolence of those who want to claim him', and when the three years were up, his profession was secure—unless he later left the community, in which case he returned to slavery with his former master.[31] From the slave's point of view, becoming a monk was a suspension of his servile status, not a cancellation of it. For an abbot, the whole process was a complex one of negotiation, perhaps also of reconciliation, between master and slave.

The Church made no attempt to challenge slavery as an institution. Church leaders, from St Paul to Gregory the Great, regarded it as divinely ordained and an opportunity for spiritual growth.[32] By the time of Benedict, slaves were being treated a little better than in previous centuries and some of this improvement may have been due to the Christian consciences of individual slave-owners, but there had, in any case, been a tendency to treat slaves more paternally, to value their opinions, and to give them work that suited their abilities. In Italy, most slaves were by then employed in domestic work, where their lives were relatively comfortable, though still tinged with fear of the abuse they might suffer at the whim of a master or mistress. It is almost certain that some of the experimental monastic households of the Roman elite had slaves working as slaves; the ascetic lifestyle of Paulinus of Nola, for example, would have been impossible without slaves to serve the meals or heat the bath water. There was absolutely no possibility of such an arrangement at Monte Cassino; even the menial jobs were shared. Benedict made it clear that there should never be any distinction in the monastery between a monk born free and a monk coming from slavery (*RB* 2.18) for, as St Paul had said, whether slave or free, we are all one in Christ (Gal 3:28). It is impossible to know whether this affected Benedict's thinking about slavery per se, but in practice he and his community were firmly egalitarian.

Social hierarchy was reflected in many aspects of public life. The different ranks among the aristocracy had titles—such as *perfectissimus*—that advertised their pedigree and income. The *curiales* ranked themselves according to the size and importance of their towns. Lawyers looked down on merchants

The Monastery in the World

who lived merely on 'profit'. In the amphitheatres the elite sat in front, with the commoners ranked in rows behind them. In the courts, the same crime carried a small fine for the elite, a heavy one for the peasants and a flogging—or worse—for the slaves. At communal celebrations, when food was handed out and cash grants distributed, the poorest citizens got least, even when their need was greatest. The sense of hierarchy affected inter-personal relations of every kind. Casual violence, such as slapping and punching, was commonly meted out to social inferiors. Even among commoners, it was normal to 'deal with equals as equals, take advantage of those below you when possible, [and] defer to those above you always'.[33] This encouraged a culture of pretence and dishonesty, of exaggerated manners and excessive servility, of bribing the strong and neglecting the weak.

People learnt the signs of rank from an early age, so that their judgement of others was instinctive and automatic. When Benedict's monks entered the monastery they had to learn to resist their cultural conditioning. They had to learn how, on their occasional forays beyond the monastery gate, they could move around in the world without acting in the world's ways (*RB* 4.20). Above all, when they were at home in the monastery they had to learn how to treat all their brothers 'as Christ' without any of the old patterns of discrimination.

8

The Community at Home

THE MOST IMPORTANT RELATIONSHIP in the monastery was the one between the abbot and the monk. The abbot was the head of the monastic household, in religious and ethical matters, as well as in the management of property and social relations. His responsibilities flowed into every corner of life and created ripples of obligation in return.

Benedict said that the abbot of a monastery should be called *dominus et abbas* (*RB* 63.13). In using the word *abba* for 'father', Benedict pointed his monks towards the tradition of the Desert Fathers and, beyond that, to the New Testament (e.g. *RB* 2.3 and Rom 8:15). The word *dominus*, on the other hand, would have had a very contemporary resonance. Everyone in the community would have connected it immediately with the role of the household head—the *dominus*—in the society around them and in which they had grown up. Benedict generally avoided using the word *paterfamilias*, the normal term for the biological father of a family, but at various points in the *Rule* (e.g. *RB* 2.24) he made it clear that he expected the abbot to have a fatherly role.[1]

It was common in the Roman household for the *dominus* and the *paterfamilias* to be the same person, with the two roles merged into one. Benedict himself combines these roles when he says that monks should look to 'the father of the monastery' for their material needs (*RB* 33.5). The *dominus* owned and controlled all property belonging to the household or created by its members. When monks entered the monastery they were expected to give up all their possessions (*RB* 58.24 and 59.3) and to depend on the abbot for clothing and anything else they might need (*RB* 33.1–5 and 55.17–19). In the traditional Roman household, the *paterfamilias* had the power of life or death over another member, a power that was seldom used and one that Benedict would not have wanted to reproduce in the monastery, but an echo of it can be seen in his statement that a monk 'will have no power even over his own body' (*RB* 58.25). Both the household head and the abbot could expect 'prompt obedience' (*RB* 5.1) and could enforce this with a range of punishments, from whipping (*RB* 23.5, 71.9) to expulsion from the community (*RB* 28.6).

In practice, the severity of the Roman *paterfamilias* seldom, if ever, came close to the traditional stereotype; authority was often softened by love and indulgence. Roman homilies on the behaviour of parents and estate owners recommended 'dutiful and gentle affection of parents towards children'[2] and a combination of affection and justice in dealings with slaves. Filial piety, the conventional response to parental

The Community at Home

authority, was also a complex pattern of behaviour; instead of mere obedience and submission, it often demonstrated real love and respect for parents and affectionate treatment of all family members.[3] Benedict picked up these nuances in his discussion of the relationship between abbot and monks. Monks, he wrote, ought to show sincere and humble love to their abbot (*RB* 72.10). The abbot, for his part, must love everyone equally (*RB* 2.22) but manifest this in different ways, as appropriate—sometimes encouraging, sometimes stern and demanding, but also showing 'the loving affection of a father' (*RB* 2.24). The abbot should be 'discerning and moderate' (*RB* 64.17) and 'strive to be loved rather than feared' (*RB* 64.15). Above all, the abbot had a responsibility for the moral and spiritual leadership of the community, showing forth 'all good and holy things by his words and even more by his deeds' (*RB* 2.12) for 'he will have to render an account on the Day of Judgement for all these souls, in addition, of course, to his own' (*RB* 2.38).

This broad responsibility for the spiritual welfare of all one's dependents had always been part of the traditional role of the household head. The Church had placed fresh emphasis on this during the fifth century, arguing that morally upright leadership would create more harmonious households, which would in turn contribute to a more harmonious society. The same point was taken up in homilies on household management which were written in the fifth and sixth centuries. These homilies urged

Saint Benedict in his Community

household heads to avoid immodest behaviour; to train their tongues to speak no evil, swear no oaths and avoid gossip; to inculcate good habits that would make the whole of life virtuous; and to encourage a spirit of true humility in which everyone in the community would 'anticipate one another with honour' and 'love to serve as subjects'.[4] If the head of the household was a *domina*—that is, a widow or an unmarried woman—it was argued that she, no less than her male equivalent, should strive to be seen as a parent, acting always in a spirit of *pietas*—or dutiful reverence, the core virtue of the Roman household—so that she would be regarded as a spiritual exemplar and as a mother rather than a taskmistress. For example, Gregoria, a female landowner of the early sixth century, was urged to 'be a model for all your servants'; 'let them see your eyes continually lifted to the heavens ... By this model you will secure your own salvation and that of those over whom you have been worthy to rule'.[5]

There is no evidence of a direct connection between any of these homilies and Benedict's *Rule*. In any case, the first of Benedict's two chapters on the abbot (*RB* 2) is lifted almost entirely from the *Rule of the Master* (*RM* 2), so we have to wonder if it was the Master who had picked up maxims from the contemporary discussion about the role of the Christian household head. Benedict's endorsement of so much of *RM* 2 does suggest that he, no less than the Master, was happy to accept some of the ideas that were in general circulation. His second chapter on the abbot (*RB*

The Community at Home

64), which was his own composition, gives a clearer view of his use of sources. Benedict's portrait of the abbot (*RB* 64.7–19) contains several quotations from the Bible and references to Cassian and Augustine, intermingled with directives that were similar in content, if not quite in phraseology, to the precepts that were being urged upon the household heads of the time.[6] It must surely be the case that Benedict's depiction of the abbot was drawn in outline from his own experience and his knowledge of Christian households, both in theory and in practice. His portrait was then given weight by reference to monastic authors and refined by reference to Scripture. It therefore seems clear that the *Rule* was derived in part from the cultural context of its author and was not simply developed from Benedict's reading of the Scriptures or inherited from the monastic tradition.

Benedict appointed subordinates to assist him in the daily management of the community. When the community grew large it was convenient to divide the monks into groups, each led by a dean (*RB* 21.1–2). There were precedents for the appointment of deans in early monastic rules, but the main reason why Benedict used them must surely have been the topography of the Subiaco site; the community had to be split between a dozen priories and it was necessary to give each priory a leader. At Monte Cassino there were probably not many more than thirty or forty monks in total and deans would have been unnecessary. Benedict also appointed a deputy, the prior, to do whatever was delegated to him (*RB* 65.16). Benedict disliked having to make such an appointment, but it was probably forced on him by the managerial duties that accumulated at Monte Cassino.

Benedict expressed himself very forcefully on the danger of deans and priors becoming puffed up with their new status. He thought this was particularly likely when abbot and prior were appointed by the same people, so that the prior might assume that he was exempt from the abbot's authority (*RB* 65.3–6). This seems to have been exactly what Benedict himself did when he appointed both leaders at Terracina (*Dialogue* 22.1). Did something go wrong at Terracina as a result? Was the situation any more harmonious at Subiaco? When Benedict left there, he reorganised the community—presumably concentrating the remaining monks into fewer priories—and promoted the deans into priors (*Dialogue* 8.5). It may be that, with their abbot at least three days journey away, one of the priors began to fancy himself as *primus inter pares* and triggered a bout of competition and factionalism. Perhaps the angry tone of the *Rule* (65.2–10) is the result of bitter experience, made worse by Benedict's realisation that it was his own decisions that had caused these difficulties to arise.

Benedict also appointed a small cadre of monks, known as seniors or *senpectae*, who had the qualities of wisdom and discretion that enabled them to hear confessions or have a quiet word with brothers who were falling into error (*RB* 27.2 and 46.5–6).

The Community at Home

Within the Roman household, the autocracy of the *paterfamilias* was circumscribed in various ways, so that the reality of life was different from the legal norm. One brake on the father's power was the *consilium* or council of close family members. The *paterfamilias* was not obliged to take the council's advice, but he might not get legal backing for his actions if he did not consult it. Benedict had a *consilium* in the monastery (*RB* 3); the whole community participated in it when important matters were under discussion, otherwise only the seniors were involved. The abbot was expected to ponder the brothers' advice, but the final decision was his alone. He was urged to listen carefully, even to the most junior members of the community (*RB* 3.3), and make proper allowance for the character and intelligence of each individual (*RB* 2.32).

The *consilium* must have been a major influence on Benedict as he grew into his own role as abbot. In the very early years of the community, when the first monks were gathering around Benedict in the Subiaco forest, the governance of the community must have gone through a process of improvisation and experiment. No doubt Benedict took the lead, but some of his suggestions must have been debated in a *consilium* and the ultimate consensus must have owed much to the monks' inherited belief in Roman social norms.

Within the monastery, the autocracy of the abbot was moderated by his concern for each monk as an individual. This is shown — paradoxically — by the system of discipline and punishment laid down in the *Rule*. To the modern reader this may appear harsh and legalistic, but a monk of late antiquity would have thought it natural to be living under a legal code. The important point, however, is that the application of this code involved discussions between the offender and his superiors, so that the offender understood why it was necessary for him to follow the *Rule* and the superiors understood why he found it difficult to comply.

Benedict gives a synopsis of the disciplinary process in *RB* 23. The offender was to be admonished privately, not once but twice, and then reprimanded in public. If necessary, he would then suffer two levels of internal excommunication which Benedict amplifies in *RB* 24 and 25: the offender had to suffer increasing degrees of exclusion from meals and the oratory and the severance of contact with other members of the community. The final stages of discipline, amplified in *RB* 27 and 28, were under the guidance of the abbot and included corporal punishment and expulsion from the monastery. Benedict says that the abbot should follow the example of the Good Shepherd in giving priority to the rescue of one wayward member of the flock; alternatively, the abbot could be likened to a wise physician, who tries every kind of ointment and medicine before reluctantly deciding to amputate. Even then, Benedict gives an offender two opportunities to reform and return (*RB* 29). Discipline and punishment there had to be, but the abbot was,

The Community at Home

throughout this process, more of a counsellor than an autocrat.

This attitude to punishment was broadly consistent with the customs of secular society. The aims of Roman punishment were reform and deterrence and they often involved a challenge to the offender's sense of honour, a spur to make him preserve his honour by changing his ways. Benedict tried to accomplish this in the monastery, first, by a quiet meeting between the offender and the *senpectae* and then with a public rebuke that served as a deterrent to others. This was a process that was consciously modelled on Christ's teaching (Mt 18:15–17) but it must also have been shaped by Benedict's experience of managing the band of followers that gathered around him in the Subiaco forest.[7] Excommunication for various offences had been recommended by the Pauline epistles, by Cassian and by other monastic writers and it would have been quite familiar in the worship of the early Church, where penitents were seated apart from the rest of the congregation.

Corporal punishment had been prescribed by some of the earlier monastic rules and by recent councils of the Church, but it was such a common feature of the Roman legal system that its presence in the monastery is not in the least surprising. In secular society beating and whipping were mainly inflicted on children and slaves, as it was assumed that neither of these categories of people were fully rational or had a sense of honour to which one could appeal. Benedict prescribed it as a late stage of discipline for monks who seemed unable to understand the need for reform, evidence that their capacity for rational behaviour was no better than that of children. He also thought corporal punishment was an appropriate way—though not the only way—to discipline boys (*RB* 30.3). For instance, mistakes in the oratory, for which an adult monk would have to make public satisfaction to the rest of the community, would, in the case of a boy who had failed to learn a psalm by heart, lead to a whipping, in the same way that a Roman schoolboy would be whipped for failing to learn his lessons (*RB* 45). The general upbringing of children in the monastery was everyone's responsibility; whether this gave everyone the right to beat a child is not clear, but Benedict insisted that the discipline of children should be moderate and reasonable (*RB* 70.5) and that nobody ought to flare up angrily at a child, as a *paterfamilias* might legitimately do in his own household.

The *Rule's* disciplinary code was designed to protect the monastic community from internal or external disruption. Benedict was very severe on anything that led to factionalism: grumbling, which was, in part, an attempt to gain sympathy and win allies; gossiping, which so often degenerated into criticism of others; and finding fault and taking sides, both verbally and physically (*RB* 34.7, 48.18, 69.1, 70.2). He wrote a whole chapter (*RB* 70) against physical violence, not because he feared his monks would be short-tempered but because he wanted to outlaw the slapping and shoving that occurred in the secular world. Benedict tried to protect the community from external attachments that might disrupt its focus on the work of God, such as gifts from relatives or news of events in the outside world (*RB* 54.1–2, 67.5). Above all, he wanted to preserve the integrity of the divine offices and the common meals, the most important events of the monastic day. A monk who arrived late or disrupted them in some other way was forced to sit separately and make satisfaction by prostrating himself in front of the whole community. This was a challenge to the offender's sense of honour; it also deprived him of his normal place in the communal hierarchy, which made life problematic for him in a number of ways.

This hierarchy operated throughout the community at the level beneath the abbot and his deputies. The monks were ranked according to the day and the hour at which they had entered the monastery (*RB* 63.7–8). The abbot might vary this order to recognise special merit or impose a penalty, but otherwise each monk's place in the hierarchy followed automatically from the precise time of his entry into the community. Each monk was simply a junior or senior in relation to another.

Benedict probably borrowed this system from the rules of the monasteries of Egypt.[8] There were important practical reasons for establishing a hierarchy of this kind. An order of precedence was necessary for the smooth running of daily life — to show, for example, whose turn it was to lead psalms in the oratory — and this system of ranking was one that the monks could easily recognise and operate. It was essential that no trace of social status from the outside world crept into it. It was also essential to meet such a danger head-on. It was not enough to exhort the monks to treat their brothers as 'one in Christ' (Gal 3:28) and then wait for worldly ideas of status to wither away; the monks had to be forced to act upon new principles which would gradually nullify the old. Benedict's system of ranking was a constant reminder to the monks to reject the social values that had governed their lives in the secular world.

In their daily interactions, seniors were to be addressed as 'reverend father' and juniors as 'brother', whatever the titles they might have had before coming to the monastery and whatever their chronological age; Benedict was adamant that time of arrival was the essential criterion of rank. Benedict also discouraged the use of personal names with their various social connotations (*RB* 63.11–12). A junior was to rise and offer his seat to a senior, whereas in the world outside the monastery an older man would always have given his place to a younger one if he judged the latter to be socially superior. Whenever the monks met as they went about their business, juniors were to ask seniors for a blessing, even if the senior had once been inferior to them in the world outside.

It is a paradox that Benedict used a system of ranking to promote a spirit of egalitarianism. Nevertheless, there is no doubt that that was his aim. Towards

The Community at Home

the end of his *Rule* he wrote about the 'good zeal' of monks, a chapter (*RB* 72) which encapsulates the virtues of a good community. Apart from the position of the abbot, no trace of hierarchical distinction remains; seniority has disappeared into reciprocity and differences of rank have dissolved into mutual support and love.

In the secular world, it was wealth that underpinned most social distinctions. Benedict was adamant that monks should not keep personal possessions when they entered the monastery (*RB* 58.24), receive gifts from outside (*RB* 54.1), or retain a link with their family property. He did not want any of the brothers to be lured away from the monastery by the prospect of a substantial inheritance. A more pressing problem was a postulant's *peculium*, the allowance customarily given by wealthy fathers to their sons, which gave young men some financial independence and enabled them to make their own way in the world. Benedict wanted the capital of the *peculium* to follow the postulant into the monastery as a donation, but since the *peculium* remained, in law, the property of the *paterfamilias*, the father also had to be involved in the gift (*RB* 59.4–5). Benedict presented this option to donors as a way of fulfilling their obligation to give alms to society and thereby winning a heavenly reward.[9]

Instead of having possessions of their own, each monk was to depend on the father of the monastery, the abbot, who would provide them with whatever they needed (*RB* 33.5, 34.1). Benedict was not just concerned about the equitable distribution of monastic property; he also wanted to stamp out the idea that anyone might have a private right over any part of it (RB 33.6) — an idea that could easily creep into community life if someone insisted, for example, on sitting in a favourite chair or having a particular bowl set at his place in the refectory.

To give up the very idea of private ownership was a lesson in humility, especially for monks from wealthy families. But although a monk no longer had the means to look after himself, this did not mean that his individual requirements were overlooked. The abbot was to provide everything necessary and take into account 'the weaknesses of those in need' (RB 55.21). In all his domestic arrangements, Benedict was moderate, practical and sensitive to differing circumstances. In his chapter on the monks' wardrobe (RB 55) Benedict prescribes a change of clothes to allow for laundering, thicker clothes for winter and extra garments if local conditions made that necessary.[10] Every monk was to have a tunic, similar to those worn by most Italian men, a garment worn next to the skin, reaching to the knees and fastened with a girdle; a cowl, a thicker, outer garment with a hood attached; and a scapular, rather like an apron hanging from the shoulders, to protect the wearer while he was at work. Monks who travelled away on business and needed to ride a mule were given a pair of drawers to protect the thighs. Heavy boots were provided for outdoor work and stockings or fur linings to keep the feet warm in winter. Benedict did not insist on clothes of a particular fabric or colour; he just said they should be whatever was available locally at a reasonable cost. This indicates that the clothes were not made in the monastic workshop but were purchased from local weavers and tailors, perhaps in Aquinum, a town which may have been a centre of woollen manufacturing and was known for the production of cheap red and purple dyes. Those same colours must have been worn by many of the local people. Since Benedict recommends that the community should do likewise, we probably ought to imagine the monks clad in cowls from that colour spectrum, a rust-red, perhaps, or a dull purple—something that was both dignified and dark enough to conceal smudges of dirt.[11]

Benedict's moderation was also on display in matters connected with diet. He thought the monks' food should be 'enough', but should also include a choice of dishes to allow for individual preferences (RB 39.1). The ration of bread should be generous—'a full pound' (RB 39.4). Benedict wryly confessed to having difficulty in fixing a ration of wine—it was too high to be ideal, but might be too low to be enforceable—so, he said, 'let us agree at least about this that we should not drink our fill, but more sparingly' (RB 40.6). In any case, the abbot should be prepared to vary the diet or the timing of meals so that monks were adequately refreshed from their labour in every season.

Work in the kitchen and the refectory involved all members of the community, working as equals and doing jobs that would have been well below their status in the world outside. Two helpers were appointed to the kitchen each week, and no one was excused unless they had other monastic business to attend to. They prepared and served the meals, washed utensils and towels and washed the feet of all the other brothers. It was here, where cooperation and adaptability were required and where individual foibles were likely to be most irritating, that the 'good zeal' of monks was put most severely to the test.

Work in the kitchen must have begun in the darkness before dawn when the two helpers groped their way to the fireplace, rummaged in the ashes for a glowing ember and revived the fire with twigs and straw. The next job was to grind flour. In Subiaco the grinding was probably done with a hand quern, which consisted of two stones fitting closely together on a vertical axis, the upper one revolved with a handle. The work was monotonous and tiring and required frequent changes of position as one arm tired and the other took over to keep the millstone revolving. When enough flour had been produced, it was mixed with water to make a heavy dough, placed in an earthenware crock and pushed into the fire to cook. At Monte Cassino bread-making was on a larger scale in a specialised bakery (*RB* 46.1) and the flour would have been ground between millstones powered by a donkey plodding slowly round in circles. It is unlikely that the bakery was used every day because of the labour involved in collecting firewood for the ovens; bread was probably made occasionally in large quantities, allowed to dry and harden, and then softened again with water to make it edible.[12]

Next came the preparation of vegetables and herbs. In many cases these were tougher and more fibrous than their modern equivalents and required heavy pounding with a mortar and pestle, another exhausting job. Among the vegetables eaten were roots such as onions, garlic and carrots; leaf vegetables such as cabbage, lettuce, broccoli and beets; legumes such as beans; and a wide variety of herbs. Turnips were common because they kept well and could be used to add bulk to the diet in years when the wheat crop failed. It can safely be assumed that most vegetables were grown on Monte Cassino or in the countryside nearby. These were the raw materials which monks in the kitchen had to peel, pound and boil. Much of their time would have been spent on the preparation of relishes to relieve an otherwise monotonous diet. For example, a few heads of garlic, some handfuls of parsley, rue and coriander, might be pounded in a mortar with sheep's cheese, olive oil, a little salt, and a drop of vinegar to produce a creamy paste. It is probable that, in certain seasons, this was one of the 'cooked' dishes on the refectory table. A significant part of the diet may have been slices of hard bread smeared with a savory relish, similar to the *bruschetta* of modern Italian cuisine.[13]

Altogther work in the kitchen was tedious, tiring and messy—a sharp lesson in humility for monks who had come from aristocratic families and whose slaves had always done the grinding, pounding and cooking.

Food supply and dietary balance were often discussed by Roman agronomists, since these were matters of importance for estate owners who needed to keep their workers fit and healthy. Benedict shows a similar concern for his monks. Wheat was the staple foodstuff of all Romans, rich or poor, and was eaten either as bread or as porridge; the former seems to have been the norm in Monte Cassino. Olive oil, another staple, goes without mention in the *Rule*, but was certainly present in the kitchen as it was an ingredient in almost all Roman cooking. The consumption of wine, the third of the trinity of Roman staples, was calculated by Benedict at the rate of one *hemina* per person per day. It is not clear what this amounts to in modern units of measurement, but half a bottle of wine seems a reasonable guess.[14] Consumption would have increased when summer heat and hard labour brought on a heavy thirst, especially if it was added to water to make the water taste less brackish. It is most unlikely that vines were grown on Monte Cassino itself, so supplies probably came from a vineyard on the plain, or perhaps from the community at Terracina. The total consumption of wine must have been enormous, the equivalent of at least 350 modern bottles every month. Not surprisingly, Gregory's *Dialogue* describes wine being delivered to the monastery in casks (*Dialogue* 18.1).

Benedict ruled out the consumption of meat from four-footed animals (*RB* 39.11) except when a more

The Community at Home

nourishing diet was needed for the sick and for the young boys in the community. Like many rural households, the monastery would have had a flitch of cured ham hanging in its storeroom, from which slices would have been cut as required. It is not clear whether Benedict intended his prohibition of meat to extend to chicken, but since he does not expressly forbid it, it seems more likely than not that it was eaten occasionally.[15]

It is certain that many foods other than the staples were also consumed; monks, no less than agricultural workers, needed a balanced intake of proteins, minerals and calories.[16] Sheep's cheese was a common ingredient in all kinds of dishes, sometimes even in bread. Most rural communities kept chickens, so the monks would have eaten eggs; and when the hens stopped laying they probably went into the pot. Honey was the only sweetener available and would have come from wild bees in the forest or from hives. A wide variety of foods could be gathered from nature, such as chestnuts, mushrooms, blackberries and wild asparagus, and these were sometimes served in a bowl of fresh fruit and vegetables alongside the cooked dishes at each meal. On some occasions the monks' table may have looked like the repast, described by Ovid, which two elderly peasants spread before honoured visitors: a dessert of 'nuts, a mixture of figs and wrinkled dates, plums and fragrant apples in shallow baskets and black grapes, freshly gathered'.[17] In some seasons of the year the monks' diet would have been both varied and healthy. At other times—and especially in years of bad harvest—there must have been long periods when the stew was little more than boiled turnips—a thin gruel to soften the bread—and the bread itself was bulked out with ground acorns or chestnuts.[18]

Feeding the community was easy in the months between May and September when most edible plants, both wild and cultivated, came to fruition. The problem came in winter and early spring when the monks—like all Italian households—had to rely on their stores. For this reason horticultural handbooks were full of advice on the preservation of food.[19] Grain was carefully cleaned to remove weevils and other pests; apples were laid in rows in a dry cellar; fleshy fruits were either pickled in brine, vinegar or honey or dried in the sun and buried in chaff; beans were shelled from their pods, dried and stored in air-tight jars; cheese was coated with wax and hung from the rafters; even lettuce could be preserved by washing in brine, steeping with fennel and leek, and then stored in brine and vinegar—a complicated process that must have tried the patience of the most saintly of monks.

All of these activities were supervised by the cellarer. Not surprisingly, Benedict devotes a whole chapter (*RB* 31) to his character and duties. He should be wise and mature, not gluttonous, unfair, dilatory or wasteful (*RB* 31.1). He needed to plan months ahead, know when and where food could be gathered or purchased, and have ready the salt, the vinegar, the chaff and the jars to store it in. He had to follow the abbot's instructions, but in a multitude of minor practical matters he would have needed to use his own discretion. He would have had to give a stream of orders to his helpers—so he should not be excitable or offensive, but ready to explain what needed to be done and able to save a situation when things went wrong. The cellarer had to show great foresight, give endless attention to detail and be calm and lucid in handling his kitchen staff—a truly exacting responsibility. Indeed, Benedict says he needed to be 'like a father to the whole community' (*RB* 31.2), for he held their lives in his hands. If he did not stock the cellar adequately for the winter, the community would starve.

His discretion was put still further to the test by the fact that most remedies for ailments were dietary ones. He had to care for the sick 'with all compassion', said Benedict (*RB* 31.9). The cellarer needed to have diagnostic skills and a supply of special diets in the store room. He also had to go to the additional trouble of serving the sick in the infirmary (*RB* 36.10). At the same time he would have had to realise that some monks might be less ill than they claimed; did that querulous brother really need a special diet to soothe his dyspepsia or was he just tired of turnip stew? He 'should not upset him by showing contempt', said Benedict, but refuse him 'with reasons modestly presented' (*RB* 31.7).

The cellarer would have monitored the supply of olive oil very carefully, for it was used every day for cooking. No wonder he was so reluctant to give it away in times of famine (*Dialogue* 28.1–2). The community seems to have produced at least some of the oil it needed. Olive trees would have been dotted about on the slopes of the mountain and no doubt the community owned groves of trees down on the plain. When ripe, the olives were put through a machine that tore the flesh off the kernel and the resulting mash then went into a heavy press which squeezed the oil into vats. The vats had to be left to settle so that the oil rose to the surface and a watery waste, known as *amurca*, sank to the bottom. The settlement process was repeated three times, with the oil skimmed off the top and the *amurca* drained off the bottom, until the oil was pure. The monks had to be alert; if the *amurca* was left too long it began to ferment, pushing the oil up over the rim of the vat. Something of this kind seems to lie behind the story of a vat, covered over and assumed to be empty, which began to ooze oil over its rim just at a moment when the monastery's stocks of oil were exhausted (*Dialogue* 29.1).

Benedict said that the cellarer, above all, should be humble (*RB* 31.13). Benedict did not want the weight of responsibility to make him arrogant; neither did he want his management of the cellar to lead to pretentions in other parts of community life. Benedict did not want any of the officers of the monastery to exceed their specified roles, undermine the abbot's authority and depart from the *Rule*. It was essential to preserve the *Rule's* system of ranking, one that not only eliminated inherited status from outside the monastery but prevented acquired status from growing up within it. Benedict did not want hierarchies of holiness or physical prowess; he did not want a monk who was naturally reserved and pious to be thought superior to one who was naturally more extrovert; he did not want someone who had memorised the entire Old Testament to be thought a better monk than someone who remembered only the Psalms; he did not want monks in the workshop to become conceited about their skilfulness or monks who were strong enough to bring in the harvest to be valued more than those who could only gather olives. All monks were simply senior or junior to each other, depending on their times of entry into the community, and everyone must offer blessings or deference accordingly.

Manual labour filled the daylight hours, apart from the offices, the meals and the time set aside for reading, and sometimes the monks' work made their physical attendance at these activities impossible (*RB* 50). Having to share in such work was a levelling influence on monks from aristocratic families, for the upper ranks of Roman society regarded manual labour and handicrafts as demeaning, whereas Benedict regarded them as a natural element of monastic life.

Much of the work was silent and solitary, allowing the words of scripture to echo in the minds of the monks and to flower into prayer. Every day monks would have been sent out alone to tend to herbs or fruit trees on the flanks of the mountain. Others would have made a longer trek into the forests on the mountains behind Monte Cassino, to return with baskets of berries, sacks of nuts or bundles of firewood tied to their backs. Some of the monks went down into the valley to work on the monastery's estate. 'They were indeed a crowd of solitaries', wrote a monk of a later generation, after watching his brothers at work in the fields; 'under the rule of silence ordered by reason, the valley became a desert for each of the many men who dwelt there ... thanks to unity of spirit and the rule of silence, in an ordered crowd of men the order safeguards the solitude of each man's heart'.[20]

9

Ways of Prayer

FAITHFUL CHRISTIANS had always aspired to a life of unceasing prayer. Many households in Italy gathered to pray at significant moments in their daily routine: in the morning, at mealtimes and when lamps were lit at dusk. Some would also pray at the third, sixth and ninth hours of the day and hold vigils at night before important festivals.[1] Wealthy families built chapels in their villas, or at least set aside a room for religious observances, and it is likely that Benedict was brought up in a household of this kind. Most families, however, would have found it hard to keep a sacred space in a tiny dwelling where many different activities crowded in upon each other. When he set up his monastery, Benedict insisted that the oratory should be used for nothing else but prayer and worship (*RB* 52.1).

These little ceremonies were probably quite simple; in most cases, the members of the household stood together, joined in a recitation of the Lord's Prayer, a canticle and a text such as the Beatitudes, and then offered intercessions of their own. Psalmody was gradually added. Psalm 140 (141) was an early favourite for the evening office, with its evocation of prayer rising like incense at an evening sacrifice, and Psalm 62 (63) became an established part of the morning ritual.[2] The liturgy for wealthier households may have been more elaborate if they had monks as spiritual advisers—as Dionysius Exiguus was to the Anicii—or if monks became ascetic residents in an aristocratic household, as sometimes happened.

A similar process of liturgical development took place in the *tituli* and other churches of Rome, forming what came to be known as the 'cathedral tradition'. This liturgy continued some of the elements of household prayer and was used at the two daily offices of Lauds and Vespers. It involved a greater use of psalms; Psalm 50 (51) and the psalms of praise (148–50) were normally sung at dawn. The offices also used easily memorised hymns and responses, as well as elaborate ceremonials with candles and incense, especially at the 'resurrection vigil' which took place early on Sunday mornings. Church leaders such as Ambrose of Milan and Caesarius of Arles encouraged lay people to learn psalms, hymns and chants so that they could participate more fully in the services, and these forms of devotion must surely have found their way back into household prayers as well. The monasteries of Rome followed a similar liturgy at Lauds and Vespers, but added the day-time offices of Terce, Sext and None, night-time vigils, and a more complete psalmody.

Benedict borrowed from both of these Roman traditions when shaping a liturgy for his community (*RB* 16). But he borrowed more widely still, bringing together an extremely eclectic collection of practices from East and West, 'a veritable cosmopolitan gathering house'.[3] He also made significant alterations to this material. He abolished all-night vigils so that his monks got an adequate amount of sleep; he redistributed the psalms between the various offices to avoid repetition, while at the same time ensuring that the entire psalter was chanted every week; and he included a theological commentary among the readings at Vigils (*RB* 9.8). He included 'Ambrosian' hymns at Vigils, Lauds and Vespers, a more extensive use than in other liturgies.[4] While the links between Benedict and his various priestly and monastic contemporaries are the most obvious sources of the liturgy used at Monte Cassino, we should not forget that this liturgy also had roots which reached back to the long and continuing tradition of household prayers among the laity.

There is one conspicuous absentee from Benedict's *horarium* of offices: the Mass. This has troubled many commentators and some have tried — rather too hard, perhaps — to interpret the *Rule* in a way that brings the *horarium* into conformity with the Church's belief in the centrality of the Mass. The problem arises, in part, from the changing use of the word *missa*. It would soon come to mean 'the Mass' but in Benedict's time it was only just beginning to acquire that meaning;[5] it more commonly referred to 'the dismissal', the concluding section of congregational worship in the early Church, which was accompanied by prayers and blessings. This is clearly the sense in which Benedict uses *missa* on four occasions when he is discussing the day offices—for example, at the end of Compline (*RB* 17.10), when the monks would have been ready to go silently to bed, not assemble for Mass—and it is the most likely meaning of two other uses of *missa* (at *RB* 35.14 and 60.4).[6] It is also an appropriate translation of *RB* 38.2, where Benedict is describing the sequence of events between the midday office and the main meal of the day. Here most translators prefer 'Mass' because *missa* closely follows the word *domenica* (Sunday). However, the two words are in different sentences—and in subordinate clauses at that—and both sentences are in a chapter about the duties of the reader at mealtimes. Either Benedict has chosen an extraordinarily oblique way of referring to the Mass, or it is too flimsy a basis on which to conclude that Mass was celebrated each Sunday in his monastery. Such a translation of *RB* 38.2 leaves Benedict guilty of sowing confusion by using the same word for two important, but completely different, parts of his community's worship. It also leaves unexplained the contrast between his care in describing the content and timing of the offices and the lack of any corresponding attention to the Mass. The only logical conclusion to be drawn is that Mass was not said regularly at Monte Cassino.[7]

This does not mean that Benedict's community neglected the Eucharist. During the early years at Subiaco the monks probably went to the local church and received the sacrament from the local priest.

After the move to Monte Cassino this would hardly have been possible; the monastery was too remote and the journey to a church on the plains too arduous. The community therefore practised a simple rite of communion *extra missam*, which took place after the prayers of dismissal at the midday office and just before the main meal of the day. The monks received portions of consecrated bread, reserved from a Eucharist elsewhere, and shared a cup of wine, which the abbot blessed by immersing a morsel of the bread. Private communions of this kind were common in Christian households. They needed no priest and no liturgy; the consecrated Host was an object of veneration in its own right. Since the earliest days of Christianity, families had gathered quietly in this way to say a prayer, remember Christ's sacrifice and share the sacrament among themselves before they sat down to eat.[8] In his arrangements at Monte Cassino, Benedict was simply continuing this ancient tradition. There was was no need to describe it in the *Rule*. The community probably received its reserved sacrament from the bishop of Aquinum. He and Benedict were on good terms, so it was said, but there was not necessarily any favouritism in this arrangement; it was perfectly normal for a bishop to supply consecrated bread to another place of worship in his diocese. According to the *Dialogue* (24.2), the bread was kept in Benedict's cell and it was also used in two of his miracles.

Reservation of the sacrament for private consumption had been common among the laity for generations. In the fourth century the Church began to frown upon this because, once the consecrated Host was in private hands, people might use it as a talisman or medicine rather than as a sacrament.[9] But the Church was in no position to stamp this out; it had neither the buildings nor the clergy to offer Mass to the whole population and it therefore had to make use of reservation itself. In Rome, the bishop distributed portions of his Sunday Eucharist to the local churches—a symbol of diocesan unity—and the local churches reserved part of their own Host for deacons to distribute to the sick and any other members of the congregation who might request it. Daily weekday Eucharist was not celebrated in Rome's basilicas until well into the sixth century.

The primary obligation of Christians was therefore to join together in offering morning and evening prayer.[10] Daily Mass was not available, and the Eucharist could only be *extra missam*. For Benedict's community the *Opus Dei*, the Work of God—to which nothing must be preferred (*RB* 43.3)—was the cycle of offices.

If there was no regular Mass in the monastery there was no need to include a priest among the monks. Benedict was very cautious about introducing one; if a priest asks to join the monastery, he wrote, 'this should not be granted him too quickly' (*RB* 60.1). By starting the sentence with the word 'if' he implies that priests were not normally part of the community; and he is emphatic that, if a priest does ask to join, his application should be given careful thought. Benedict was concerned that the priestly vocation might prove to be at odds with the monastic charism. He warns in the harshest terms about the danger of monastic ideals being eroded from within, quoting Christ's words to Judas at the moment of betrayal: 'friend, for what purpose have you come'(Mt 26:50 and *RB* 60.3).

Benedict was not alone in his misgivings. Cassian, Jerome and others had warned that ecclesiastical order was incompatible with monastic life and many early monasteries, including the Master's, were resolutely lay in character.[11] During the fifth century this antipathy to clerical involvement was reciprocated by successive popes and their secretariats, who looked down on monks because they were laymen and had not risen through a clerical hierarchy. That was Benedict's concern. He was not trying to create an ecclesiastical elite for leadership and ministry; he was trying to create a new kind of community, based on love and obedience to each member and to God. He was afraid that priests who had been trained for a leadership role would expect to dominate a community of laymen. Hence his wariness about the admission of clergy and his insistence that the *Rule* must stand above everyone—monks, priests and even the abbot. In addition he would not have wanted to import any of the Church's factional disputes into the monastery, neither the theological wrangles between West and East nor the lingering resentments from the Laurentian schism.

Some of these problems could be avoided if a priest was ordained from among the existing monks. Benedict discusses this possibility in *RB* 62. The ordination would, of course, be carried out by the bishop, but the choice of ordinand was to be the abbot's; the new priest must not let ordination go to his head, must not do anything that the abbot had not ordered, and must retain his existing rank within the community unless the abbot and the other monks decided to promote him (*RB* 62.2–6). Benedict describes this as a case of an abbot having a priest ordained 'for himself' (*RB* 62.1).[12] Benedict is here establishing a priesthood similar to that on the great estates of Italy, where the landowner chose one of his retainers to be ordained, had him approved by the local bishop, and then gave him his orders. At Monte Cassino the priest would, most obviously, have been required to keep the community supplied with consecrated bread if an existing supply dried up; he would probably have celebrated Mass on feast days and reserved part of the sacrament for use at later communions. The monastery had relics of certain saints (*RB* 58.19) and there may have been rituals connected with these that the priest could perform. He may also have been required to say regular prayers over graves in the monastic cemetery. If he was one of the *senpectae*—which would have been a logical role for him—he may have been able to add a more spiritual dimension to the advice given to erring monks. Very importantly, as the abbot's man he would have been an insurance against the interference of another Florentius and against clerical pressure more generally.

Professed monks might sometimes come to the monastery from elsewhere and the community needed to be ready to take them in as long-stay visitors or permanent recruits (*RB* 61). After war broke out in Italy in 536, such people may have arrived in substantial numbers and in some distress, having experienced the destruction of their monasteries and the ravaging of their lands by rival armies. Monks who had lived in wealthy households as spiritual advisers might have become homeless if their patrons had fallen on hard times or decamped to the East. Benedict recognised that some of these men had a real commitment to their vocation and a valuable experience of it in other monasteries and, in a typically humble way, he saw this as an opportunity for his own community to learn from them.

On the other hand, some of the visitors to Monte Cassino were vagabond monks with very questionable intentions. These were the so-called gyrovagues, pure charlatans, putting on a show of hunger and holiness at the door of a monastery in the hope of a free lunch and a clean bed. An experienced porter would have recognised them at once and sent them packing.

The monastery also had a steady trickle of genuine guests. One such was Servandus, the abbot of a monastery in Campania (*Dialogue* 35.1). His monastery had been founded by Liberius, a great patrician landowner and statesman in Theoderic's administration who had founded several monasteries in the countryside south of Rome. Another of those foundations was Alatri, where Benedict and his monks had stayed on their journey from Subiaco to Monte Cassino. Benedict's connection with this group of monasteries may have led to reciprocal visits between their abbots. Another connection that seems certain was with Lucullanum, its abbot Eugippius and its scriptorium, and therefore with the network of monasteries that circulated the books that the scriptorium produced. It seems likely that Benedict was well informed about the life of other monastic communities in the region and about developments in the Church generally. Even so, it is unlikely that any of these contacts, apart from Lucullanum, had much influence on the content of the *Rule*—its intellectual origins in Cassian, the Master and Augustine are sufficient explanation of that—or that the *Rule* was an archetype of some kind of Campanian monasticism. When Benedict died, he was ignored by the Church in Italy for several generations, which shows that, apart from Gregory and his informants, there was no body of monastic opinion to champion his memory or his *Rule*.

Italy also contained a variety of smaller communities with different degrees of commitment to the ascetic life, known collectively as sarabaites. Benedict was scathing about them. Instead of holding fast to a rule, they were, he wrote, as soft as lead, changing their principles to fit whatever took their fancy (*RB* 2.6–9). He borrowed his words from the

Ways of Prayer

Master, but he had reasons of his own to condemn them; the danger of living without a rule had been forcefully brought home to him by the community at Vicovaro (*Dialogue* 3.3). Yet he may have been a bit hard on sarabaites generally; after all, he had once been something of a sarabaite himself. In his very earliest days at Subiaco he must have made many compromises and changes of direction as he groped his way towards a clearly formulated rule for his community and a role for himself as abbot.

Some small communities consisted of young men who had gathered together into ascetic households, much like the fledgling community at Subiaco. These households had placed themselves under the direction of a priest or bishop and their rule of life, though not written down, was based on biblical examples. Some of them may have been quite fertile environments for spiritual growth, while others may have succumbed to the compromises that Benedict condemned. However, it is doubtful if any of them would have provided, to Benedict's satisfaction, the long test of obedience to a rule and to a superior which he thought necessary to produce a truly monastic community.

If the households of ascetic men had little to teach the monastery, the opposite was true of their female counterparts. Monks went often from Monte Cassino to a nearby village to talk to the nuns who lived there about spiritual matters (*Dialogue* 19.1). Benedict had annual meetings with his sister Scholastica, who had been dedicated to a life of prayer since her early years (*Dialogue* 33.2). One of those meetings, which is described in the *Dialogue*, was attended by other monks and seems to have been a spiritual discussion rather than a family chat. The Church strongly disapproved of such meetings between monks and nuns. Nevertheless, relationships that were long-term and intimate—but entirely chaste—seem to have developed between monks and nuns from time to time and to have continued throughout the history of monasticism. Monks have valued the nuns' perspectives on the life of asceticism, their emotional awareness, their openness to the grace of tears, and their discernment of individual sensibilities that found no place in the *Rule*.[13]

In the previous century, communities of nuns had been a prominent part of religious life. Aristocratic women from Rome had actively promoted them, using their personal fortunes to found nunneries and lead pilgrimages to the Holy Land. By the sixth century those fortunes had been dissipated and the number of potential patrons had been reduced by the exodus of elite families to the East. Nevertheless, communities of ascetic women continued on a smaller scale. Three of Gregory the Great's aunts formed an ascetic household in Rome, where they lived on their inherited wealth in a family property. Other communities were brought together by unfortunate circumstances as well as a shared interest in a life of prayer. For example, a young abbess of Spoleto set up a convent after rebelling against her father's plans to put her into the marriage market; she was later joined by many young women of noble families.[14] Revolt against parental plans drove some young women into nunneries; so did early widowhood. On the other hand, fathers might push their daughters into a life of virginity to save themselves the trouble of arranging a marriage and the expense of a dowry; mothers might encourage their daughters to do the same in order to save them from the drudgery of household management and the dangers of childbearing. If there was no family backing, convents had to support themselves, usually by spinning, weaving and copying manuscripts. The nuns' lives were very secluded and austere, partly out of choice, partly because of straitened circumstances, and partly because of the sheer difficulty they faced in moving about in the world as single women. Whatever their situation, they led a life of prayer, psalmody and study. Some of them were extremely well informed about the theological issues of the time. Benedict and his monks would have found them challenging yet sympathetic company.

The figure of Scholastica emerges naturally from this background of female monasticism. She may have been one of those 'spiritual sisters' that monks liked to consult from time to time. On the other hand, there is some evidence that she and Benedict were siblings.[15] If so, she presumably drew upon family wealth to support herself, as Benedict had done during his studies in Rome. It is not clear whether she lived alone or in a community. If she was a solitary, she may have found shelter in an ancient basilica or a deserted classical structure near the foot of Monte Cassino; it was often the case that hermits took up residence in buildings of that kind. On the other hand, she may have been part of a community of nuns at Plombariola, a village about 5 kilometres from Monte Cassino. There was certainly a nunnery there in the eighth century and it is possible that this was a continuation of an older tradition of female asceticism in the area.[16] She was apparently well able to hold her own in a day-long discussion with Benedict and his companions, which suggests that she was well read and articulate.

Scholastica must have been an influence on Benedict throughout his life. It is tempting to believe that she ran an eye over a draft of the *Rule* and gave some of Benedict's domestic arrangements a feminine touch. However, it would be a mistake to assume that her influence on the *Rule*, if any, was always in the direction of softening its provisions; female asceticism could be very severe. If she had encouraged Benedict to write the phrase 'nothing that is harsh or hard to bear' (*RB* Prol. 46), it was also likely that she favoured the following verse, which spoke of 'a little strictness' in certain circumstances.[17]

The *Dialogue's* account of their final meeting (*Dialogue* 33.2–5), which took place in a house near the foot of the mountain, gives the impression that Scholastica was a forceful character, willing to stand up to her brother and not ashamed of displaying her emotions. When Benedict insisted on cutting short their meeting and returning to the monastery at dusk, she leant on the table and buried her head in her hands—a sign of exasperation with her brother's attachment to routine. After a few moments of intense prayer she raised her face, now wet with tears. At this point there was a clap of thunder and such a downpour of rain that a journey back to the monastery was out of the question. Somewhat grudgingly, Benedict sat down and resumed their discussion. The whole of the night was spent in conversation about the spiritual life. No doubt the *Dialogue's* account of this meeting owes something to Gregory's imagination, but it is not impossible that a meeting of this kind actually took place and that the details were etched so deeply into the memories of the other participants that they were able to report them to Gregory many years later.

On this occasion Scholastica's wishes prevailed over Benedict's. The *Dialogue* attributes this to Scholastica's prayers and the fact that 'she loved more' (*Dialogue* 33.5 from Lk 7:47, 'she loved much'), while Benedict had been distracted by thoughts of getting back to the monastery. With this deliberate misquotation from the Bible, Gregory sets up a comparison between Benedict and Scholastica—but on what point? Scholastica clearly loved her brother and it may be that Benedict did not seem to be reciprocating this love equally. At the same time, Gregory reminds us of the constant presence of God's love (1 Jn 4:8), suggesting that this may have been central to their discussion and that Scholastica had responded more to the divine illumination of this love than her brother had done.[18]

Scholastica's tears were not tears of repentance. She probably wept out of love and disappointment—love for her brother, joy at the glimpse of heaven afforded by their conversation and disappointment at its premature end. Repentance was normally the first step in compunction, as it freed the penitent to experience the piercing of the heart in other ways. Cassian had provided an analysis of these processes. True compunction was a grace and should not be forced. Tears might flow from the fear of eternal judgement or from contemplation of the sinfulness of others and the cares and hardships of the world; or tears might be a sign of irrepressible joy prompted, perhaps, by beautiful psalmody or the flash of enlightenment provided by a spiritual discussion.[19] On the other hand, compunction might be accompanied by a profound silence as the soul became lost in awe at the sight of eternal truths. The process was later summed up by Gregory the Great when he wrote that 'the perfect compunction of fear draws the intellectual soul to the compunction of love'.[20]

Benedict's understanding of compunction was very similar. Tears and sighs should, he said, accompany confession of sins (*RB* 4.57) and, in prayer generally, it was purity of heart and tears of compunction that God wished to see, rather than mere words (*RB* 20.3 and 52.4). In Lent, compunction might also be prompted by additional reading, self-denial or the reassessment of life which the season required (*RB* 49.4). This process would culminate in the joy of Easter and in spiritual longing (*RB* 49.7), thus following the trajectory of compunction from penitence to love, which Gregory would later describe.

There was no regular sacramental confession in Benedict's monastery. In this respect, Benedict held back from the changes that were going on in the wider Church, where personal confession to a priest was becoming more common among the laity and where some penitents were beginning to wear a tonsure as an outward sign of their penitential status. Monasticism and penance were increasingly conflated and it would not be long before monasteries came to be seen as natural places for penitents to live in atonement for their sins. Nevertheless, in Benedict's community, confession of sins was normally a private matter between the monk and God. Benedict tells his monks that when 'wrongful thoughts' came into their hearts, they should confess them humbly to the abbot or disclose them to a spiritual elder (*RB* 4.50, 7.44), but this was not the same as a confession of sin. It was, rather, a continuation of the Desert Fathers' custom of disclosing one's thoughts to a trusted elder as a way of cleansing the heart and being completely honest with oneself.[21]

For Benedict, the heart had many different properties and could be pierced by compunction in many different ways. The heart could listen and see; it could harbour faults and encourage virtues; it could be deceitful or truthful, recalcitrant or obedient; it was the seat of understanding as well as of the emotions; it could overflow with love. The heart was capable of making decisions and aspiring to heavenly things.[22] True purity of heart would open the way to God.

Cassian had been certain that purity of heart would allow the monk to gaze contemplatively on the divine; had not Jesus said that the pure in heart would see God (Mt 5:8)? In his *Conferences*, written in the 420s, Cassian had claimed that contemplation was achievable in this life, but it would be more or less fleeting, depending on the discipline that sustained it, a discipline that involved constant prayer, the study of scripture, the elimination of vices and the cultivation of virtues like humility and discretion.[23] Later in the century, it was being argued by writers in Gaul, notably in Arles, that contemplation might be achieved not only by monks but also by those in 'spiritual occupations', such as the governance of the Church, if those tasks were carried out with an appropriate degree of detachment and concern for the common good. Others claimed that similar illumination might come from renouncing worldly wealth and devoting it instead to the good government of an estate. One of the handbooks for estate owners advised that 'when the disciples of truth flee from human glory and sever themselves from the love of things temporal ... they may savour the things of God rather than those of men, they experience an increase in sensibility, not a decrease;

instead of losing vigour of mind, they receive the light of extraordinary understanding. They live in this world, but they detach themselves from the tumult of the world'.[24]

Benedict was more circumspect about contemplation—indeed, the word *contemplatio* does not appear in the *Rule*. Rather than Cassian's detailed account of the ascent to this form of prayer, Benedict depicts the process in a general way—the *Rule* is, after all, not a manual of prayer but a prospectus for the monastic life as a whole. The monk would pray as he lived. When considering that most intimate relationship with God, Benedict turned to the psalms: 'Lord who may dwell in your tabernacle', asked the psalmist, 'or who may rest upon your holy hill? Even he that leads an uncorrupt life' was the reply, 'and does the thing which is right and speaks the truth from his heart' (Ps 14(15):1–2; *RB* Prol. 23–6).[25] The second verse of the psalm was almost a summary of the aims of the monastic life: purity of heart and conversion of life, strengthened by obedience to one's abbot and humility before God. Then one might find a stability that offered a glimpse of what it would be like to rest upon God's holy hill.

In that stable community and in the steady rhythm of monastic life, the divine presence could be felt everywhere (*RB* 19.1) and prayer could become ceaseless. It might even develop into wordless contemplation. A monk might find, as Gregory the Great was to find in his monastery in Rome in the 580s, that the soul 'rose high above everything temporal.

It thought only about heavenly things, so that while still held in the body it had already passed beyond the prison of the flesh in contemplation'.[26]

It is impossible to know how often—or even whether—any of Benedict's monks had a contemplative experience similar to Gregory's. That would have depended upon the individual's purity of heart and the response of the Holy Spirit. In any case, the intensity of a monk's prayer was a private matter, hidden behind the humility that he was expected to practise at all times (*RB* 7.62–3). Yet Benedict does seem to have expected contemplative prayer to be within the experience of every monk. The first verse of Psalm 14(15), which he quoted in full, asked who would dwell in the Lord's tabernacle, a reference to the tabernacle—or tent—where the Israelites went to speak to the Lord during their journey through the desert to the promised land (Ex 33:7–11, 20). The tabernacle was a metaphor used in Christian literature to denote intimacy with God in contemplation; the Master had done so, and Cassian had alluded to it in a description of the many ways that God encourages us to contemplate himself.[27] Benedict promised his monks divine intimacy at the very start of the *Rule*, telling them that the path of God's commandments would open their hearts 'to a sweetness of love that is beyond words' (*RB* Prol. 49).

The same note of intimacy and joy is found in the last chapter of the *Rule*, as Benedict gives his final advice to anyone seeking the summits of monastic life (*RB* 73.9). Those lie in a place beyond anything

Ways of Prayer

that can be described in the *Rule*, a place where the 'full observance of justice' is found (*RB* 73 title), a place where 'the covenant response to the saving justice of God [is] expressed in love of God and neighbour'.[28] It is a place of contemplation and action, of loving God in prayer and worship and loving one's neighbour in the daily life of the community.

In this final chapter, Benedict also issues a challenge to each individual in the community. Anyone, he says, can learn from the teachings of Scripture and the Fathers; 'whoever you are', he goes on, you can hasten to your heavenly home with Christ's assistance and the guidance of the *Rule* (*RB* 73.2, 8). Once again, Benedict emphasises the essentially lay character of his whole monastic enterprise, rooted as it was in the ancient traditions of household worship and constant prayer. He also called to mind the old belief that all Christians — not just the members of a religious elite — could rise to perfection and that therefore the establishment of Christ's kingdom in the world was the ministry of the laity.[29] Here, Benedict issues a challenge, not just to his brother monks, but to generations to come.

Church practices, however, were moving in the opposite direction. Liturgy was becoming more clericalised, especially as the Mass was celebrated more widely and more frequently. Priestly influence in monasteries began to grow; it was becoming mandatory for monasteries in the East to choose a priest as abbot, and the same change would soon happen in the West. In Italy there was much hostility

Saint Benedict in his Community

among priests towards monks who seemed to be leapfrogging them into positions of influence. The Church was insistent on its ecclesiastical hierarchy, with increasingly powerful bishops at the top and the laity firmly at the bottom. During the sixth century the Church grew enormously in power, elaborating its canon law, enlarging its central secretariat, taking on more charitable activities and building more churches itself, rather than leaving this to wealthy benefactors. Against this background, Benedict's community can be seen as a survival of the old forms of lay piety and lay leadership, now beginning to wilt under the Church's institutional power.

The Church also increased its secular power in Italy; it became the largest landowner and the wealthiest institution. Its bishops were often the leading political figures in their cities, with a social status to match. The Church stepped into the vacuum caused by the collapse of the old forms of political power and social influence. This was largely a consequence of the war which Justinian had launched against the Italian Gothic regime. Monte Cassino was fortunate to escape destruction during the war. That may have been due to the fact that the worst of the fighting was in Rome and the north. It may also have been due to the generally good relations between Arian Goths and catholic Italo-Romans, who respected each other's places of worship, and perhaps also to respect for Benedict as a holy man. None of these considerations weighed with the Lombard warriors who swept down the Italian peninsula in the 570s, destroying Monte Cassino and most of the other monasteries as they passed. That destruction forced Benedict's community to take refuge in Rome but it ultimately sent the *Rule* out into the world.

Excursuses

Augustine, bishop and saint, was born in Thagaste, a village now known as Souk el Ahras in modern Algeria, the son of a minor bureaucrat. He was educated in local schools, then later in Carthage, where he went on to teach. At the age of 19 a book by Cicero encouraged him to philosophical enquiry, but he was attracted to the ideas of the Manichaeans rather than to orthodox Christianity. In 383 he travelled to Rome and then on to Milan, where he was a professor of rhetoric. He was much impressed by Bishop Ambrose and in 386 retired to a villa outside the city where he could engage in reading, reflection and discussion with a small group of friends. In 387 he returned to Milan and was baptised by Ambrose. A year later he returned to Thagaste, where he lived in a small community devoted to study and writing. In 391 he visited Hippo (now Annaba, in Algeria) at a time when the bishop was looking for a priest and Augustine found himself, much against his will, pushed forward for ordination by the congregation. In 395 he became bishop. He built a monastery in the garden of the church at Hippo where he and his fellows (priests and laity from various backgrounds) lived a frugal life of contemplation and prayer, based on the psalms. A nunnery was founded nearby and Augustine wrote rules for both communities. He wrote a very large number of books, notably the *Confessions* (397–400) and *City of God* (*c.* 412–26). He died in 430.

Belisarius was commander of the imperial army during Justinian's most important campaigns. In 533 he was given command of the campaign against the Vandal kingdom (covering the area that is now western Libya, Tunisia and northern Algeria), which he concluded within a year. He was equally successful in Sicily in 535. He led the imperial forces in Italy from 536

Saint Benedict in his Community

until 540. In 541 he went to the eastern front and was making headway against the Persians when plague broke out in the army and the campaign had to be halted. When Justinian also caught the plague and was briefly incapacitated, Belisarius said he would not take orders from anyone else, which Theodora took as a personal slight. She had him recalled, deposed and stripped of much of his fortune and he was only reinstated through the intercession of his wife, who was a friend of Theodora's. He led the army in Italy from 544 to 549. He then lived quietly in retirement in Constantinople until his death in 565.

Benedict and the Master. The dating and place of origin of the *Rule of the Master* (*Regula Magistri*) have been carefully considered by de Vogüé; see L. Eberle, trans., *The Rule of the Master* (Collegeville: Cistercian Publications, 1977), introduction by de Vogüé, pp. 73–83. The whole question of the relationship between Benedict and the Master has been the subject of controversy in the past, but there is now general—though not quite unanimous—agreement that the Master wrote first and Benedict drew upon him. For a recent discussion see M. Dunn, 'Mastering Benedict: monastic rules and their authors in the early medieval West' in *English Historical Review* 105 (1990), pp. 567–94 and A. de Vogüé, 'The Master and St Benedict: a reply to Marilyn Dunn' in *EHR* 107 (1992), pp. 95–103 with a rejoinder by Dunn, pp. 104–11. It has also been suggested that the *Rule of the Master* was written by Benedict himself as an early draft of the rule that now bears his name. However, I agree with those critics who say that the spirit of the two rules is so different that they could not have come from the same pen. See also Chapter 7, note 12.

The so-called 'Benedict Option'. All monastic and ascetic communities turn their backs on society to some extent, but there is a distinction to be made between those who are eager to get closer to God and those who are anxious to get further from the world. It is clear from passages in the *Rule* (e.g. Prol. 19–21) that Benedict's community belongs in the first category. In recent years it has been suggested that they belong in the second: see, for example, R. Dreher, *The Benedict Option: A Strategy for Christians in a Post-Christian Nation* (New York: Sentinel, 2017). This view sees Benedict leading his community into a kind of monastic lifeboat where they could ride out the deluge of the collapsing Roman empire. Dreher argues that similarly dedicated communities should withdraw from the political and ethical chaos of modern society. Dreher's view of Benedict flies in the face of the evidence. Firstly, Benedict did not lead a community out of society; he left it to become a solitary and a community subsequently gathered about him. Secondly, the first quarter of the sixth century was a time of relative peace and stability in Italy and the final collapse of the late Roman order did not happen until after Benedict and his community had settled at Monte Cassino. The *Rule* and the *Dialogue* are full of examples of interaction between the monastery and local society: for example, if the monks did not usually gather in their own harvest, there must have been a settled arrangement between the monastery and local agricultural labourers; if the price of goods from the monastic workshop was pegged to local prices, there must have been regular contact with the market in Casinum. If, as I have argued, Subiaco was not an economically viable site for a monastic community of this size, the move to Monte Cassino represents an attempt to get closer to the world, not further from it.

Benedict's vision. A connection between the vision of *Dialogue* 35.2–3 and the *Dream of Scipio* has been suggested by de Vogüé, *Life*, pp. 168–72, Kardong, *Life*, pp. 135–7, and many others.

It is entirely possible that Benedict had a vision of this kind and discussed it with his monks. It is also possible that the monks passed the story on to Gregory; and Gregory, not sure how to put such an experience into words, fell back upon the example provided by Cicero.

Although Benedict's vision and Scipio's dream have many similarities, there are, of course, significant differences. For

Saint Benedict in his Community

Cicero, the highest goals were social and political: 'Nothing that occurs on earth ... is more gratifying to that supreme God who rules the whole universe' than the establishment of just commonwealths; those who promoted these had a place reserved for them in heaven (III.1). For Benedict and Gregory, the highest goals were to serve Christ and share in his kingdom; the ascent of the soul of bishop Germanus, as described in the *Dialogue*, was a sign that these goals were achievable. How could one promote this outcome during one's life on earth? In the *Dream* Scipio is advised by his grandfather that the flight of the soul would be swifter 'if the soul, while it is still shut up in the body, will rise above it, and in contemplation of what is beyond, detach itself as much as possible from the body' (IX.2). In the *Dialogue* Gregory tells Peter, his interlocutor, that with even a small amount of divine light, 'everything created seems small. For the capacity of the mind is expanded by the light of interior contemplation. It is so enlarged by God that it becomes greater than the world ... For when the contemplative soul is ravished by the light of God, it is dilated. When it looks down in its elevated state it understands the insignificance of things in a way it could not when it remained below' (*Dialogue* 35.6 in Kardong's translation, pp. 132–3). But although these two recommendations of the contemplative life have many similarities, Gregory's is not derived from Cicero's. Gregory's mystical understanding was already profound and was based on his own experience.

Gregory often used light as a metaphor for contemplation, those 'chinks of contemplation' that he might, by God's grace, be allowed. He saw it as the slanting light that came narrowly through the monastery windows—mere slits on the outer face of the walls, but which splayed out into the room so that 'the inner part which receives the light is wide; because the minds of those that contemplate, although they have but a slight glimpse of the true light, yet are they enlarged within themselves with a great amplitude ... It is very little indeed that those who contemplate see of eternity;

Boethius

but from that little the fold of their minds is extended into an increase of fervour and love'. If we place Benedict within this metaphor, we can see that he not only possessed mystical illumination but did so to an unusual degree. He was not limited to chinks of light; he stood at the window itself and had a direct view of the illuminated scene. He was not limited to scattered rays inside the room that move about as clouds drift across sun or moon; he saw a single focused ray of light of great brilliance. This exceptional vision was a testimony to Benedict's great holiness.

Gregory's mysticism is discussed in detail by C. Butler, *Western Mysticism* (London: Arrow Books, 1960); my quotation is from the *Homilies on Ezekiel* quoted on p.131. There is also useful discussion of Gregory and the vision of St Benedict in B. McGinn, *The Growth of Mysticism* (New York: Crossroad, 1999), pp. 71–4 with a footnote listing modern discussions of the vision. A translation of the *Dream* can be found in Macrobius, *Commentary on the Dream of Scipio*, trans. and ed. W. H. Stahl (New York: Columbia University Press, 1990), from which my quotations have been taken, as well as translations of Cicero's *Republic*, book 6.

Boethius belonged to a branch of the eminent family of Anicii. His date of birth is not known, but it was probably in the late 470s, which would have made him a couple of years older than Benedict. His social position almost guaranteed him a high office and indeed he was made consul in 510, while still in his twenties. In 522 he was appointed Master of Offices at Theoderic's court, which gave him control over many aspects of palace life. His literary output began in about 504 with a commentary on a work by Porphyry and continued at a steady pace throughout his life. His masterpiece, *The Consolation of Philosophy*, was written while he was in prison awaiting execution. Boethius seems to have aimed his books at a select readership among the leisured aristocrats of his own social class; clearly, the young Benedict could not have read them,

Saint Benedict in his Community

though he might have done so later in life, and so might some of the young recruits to the monastery at Monte Cassino.

Bread preparation. Before the wheat was ground, it had to be pounded in a mortar with a wooden pestle to remove the husk without breaking the grain. One hand quern would have sufficed for each priory at Subiaco; there was an analogous situation in the Roman army, where one quern was issued to each unit of ten soldiers. Grinding by hand for 10–12 people would have been a long and very laborious process. Benedict specified a 'full pound' of bread per person, which was certainly more than the Roman pound (327 g) of those days. A bronze measure preserved at Monte Cassino and said to date from Benedict's time holds more than a kilo, but it has been argued that this was a measurement of dough, whereas the baked loaves would have weighed about 800 gms. If so, they would have been similar in size and weight to loaves found at Pompeii. We may be tempted to imagine the monks sitting down each day to a freshly baked white loaf, but no: the bread could have been several weeks old, an unpleasant grey colour (aristocratic households in Campania added chalk to their bread to whiten it) and full of grit from the millstones, which had a disastrous effect on people's teeth. Complaints about gritty bread are common in the literature of the time. Long intervals between bread-making were common in rural Europe until modern times. In the 1940s the most remote hamlets of Piedmont made bread in communal ovens just once a year; the bread was then hung up to dry and bits were broken off with a hammer and soaked in milk to make them edible.

Cassian. That he was one of the main influences on Benedict cannot be doubted, but how his influence should be compared with that of others is a matter of debate; for a summary of the discussion see Kardong, *Benedict's Rule*, pp. 612–15. Cassian was probably born in the early 360s, a native of Scythia (Romania), where he was given a good education in Latin by wealthy parents and became fluent also in Greek, thanks to the many

Cassiodorus

Greek influences in the region. When he was still very young, he went with his friend Germanus to a monastery in Palestine, where they met the former abbot of an ascetic community in Egypt. Intrigued by what they heard from him, the two friends set out for Egypt, where they spent some years listening to the wisdom of monks and hermits (some of these conversations are recorded in Cassian's *Conferences*). In 399 they left Egypt suddenly for Constantinople, possibly because they found themselves caught up in a controversy over the teachings of Origen. In Constantinople Cassian became a disciple of John Chrysostom and went to Rome in 404 on his behalf. In 415 he moved on from Rome to Marseille, where he spent the rest of his life and founded two monasteries, one for men and one for women. In his two great works, *The Conferences* and *The Institutes*, Cassian transmitted to a western readership some of the spiritual teaching of Origen and Evagrius and a knowledge of Egyptian monasticism in both its coenobitic and anchoritic forms. Less important is his theological work, *On the Incarnation of the Lord against Nestorius*. Cassian died about 435.

There are good studies of Cassian by P. Rousseau, *Ascetics, Authority and the Church in the Age of Jerome and Cassian* (Oxford: Oxford University Press, 1978); C. Stewart, *Cassian the Monk* (New York: Oxford University Press, 1998); and O. Chadwick, *John Cassian: A Study in Primitive Monasticism* (Cambridge: Cambridge University Press, second edn 1968). Chadwick has also written a very useful introduction to a translation of extracts from *The Conferences* by C. Luibheid (New York: Paulist Press, 1985). Both *The Conferences* and *The Institutes* have been translated by B. Ramsey (Mahwah, New Jersey: Newman Press, 1997).

Cassiodorus was born in the late 480s, the son of a wealthy landowner of Scylacium (Squillace) on the 'toe' of southern Italy. He followed his father into high office under Theoderic. In 507 he was made *quaestor*, which required him to draft the king's letters and gave him a unique insight into the king's mind and policies. In 514 he was nominated consul. After some years out of the limelight, he succeeded Boethius as *magister officiorum* (chief-of-staff) in 523 and in 533 he rose to the even higher office of praetorian prefect in the governments of Amalasuntha, Theodahad and Witigis. After the Gothic collapse in 540 he went to Constantinople, possibly as the prisoner of Belisarius; whether or not he was imprisoned, he clearly had a lot of explaining to do to Justianian and the émigré Roman community who had fled earlier to the East. He returned to his estates in Italy after the war ended and founded a monastery at Vivarium (near Scylacium). He was said to have remained active until the age of 93, which means he may have died in about 580.

Cassiodorus wrote extensively. His *Variae* are collections of the letters he wrote for successive Gothic rulers and are useful evidence for the history of the times; see *The Selected Letters of Cassiodorus: A Sixth Century Sourcebook*, ed. and trans. by M. S. Bjornlie (Oakland: University of California Press, 2020). In his retirement he wrote a commentary on the Psalms and other theological works, as well as the *Institutes of Divine and Secular Learning*, a curriculum for the education of monks. He also wrote a multi-volume history of the Goths, which now survives only in an abridgement by someone else; the aim of this work was to mediate between Romans and Goths, as Cassiodorus had done throughout his career.

Clothing. Benedict is clearly thinking of the climatic and other differences between Monte Cassino, Subiaco and Terracina. Winters on Monte Cassino can be very severe owing to the elevation, the proximity to the Abruzzi, and the monastery's exposure to northerly winds funnelling down the Liri valley. During World War II the armies that fought around the monastery had to contend with snowdrifts more than 20 feet deep and temperatures that went down to minus 30C. Winters on the coast, as at Terracina, are more temperate.

On Benedict's dress code see *RB 1980*, pp. 260–2; Kardong, *Benedict's Rule*, pp. 441–54 and H. Feiss, 'Review article: *The*

Substance of the Ephemeral: clothing in the Benedictine tradition' in *American Benedictine Review* 53 (2002), pp. 243–53. For the clothing of the population generally see K. Sessa, *Daily Life in Late Antiquity* (Cambridge University Press, 2018), pp. 187–95.

Some items may have been too mundane to mention. Sandals (of the thong variety) were ubiquitous in Italian society in summer, and since *pedules* (*RB* 55.6) can be translated in different ways, it may be best to take sandals for granted and translate *pedules* as stockings. The intriguing question, of course, is what did the monks wear under their tunics? The answer may be nothing; it is not certain that Italian men normally wore any undergarment. Since Benedict was very particular about cleanliness and since the monks normally wore the same clothes day and night, it is perhaps more likely that they wore a loin-cloth. The undergarment mentioned in *RB* 55.13 is clearly a particular garment for a particular purpose.

The codex. The codex had many other advantages over the scroll. It was possible to write on both sides of the page and for several scribes to work at once on the same volume, making book production quicker and cheaper. The codex was easier to handle and much easier to use as a reference work; for these reasons, bibles were produced as codices from the very earliest days. The most common size for a codex was 22 cm x 27 cm, with pages slightly shorter but slightly wider than a modern sheet of A4. Many codices were very much smaller than this and were obviously meant to be carried around as notebooks or as personal prayer books. Much has been written on the early history of the book and on the transition from roll to codex and from papyrus to parchment; for two wide-ranging discussions see C. Bertelli, 'The production and distribution of books in late antiquity' in R. Hodges and W. Bowden, eds, *The Sixth Century: Production, Distribution and Demand* (Leiden: Brill, 1998), pp. 41–60 and G. Cavallo, 'Between *Volumen* and codex: reading in the Roman world' in G. Cavallo and R. Chartier, eds, *A History of Reading in the West* (London: Polity Press, 1999), pp. 64–89.

Cyril of Alexandria was born in Egypt c. 378, educated in Alexandria and rose in the Church while his uncle was archbishop of the city. When his uncle died in 412, Cyril succeeded him. Cyril died in 444.

Cyril's reputation as a theologian of the highest quality has been overshadowed by his ruthlessness in dealing with his opponents and the possibility that he was linked with the violent politics of Alexandria, in particular the lynching of the Neoplationist philosopher Hypatia. Modern authors have been less ready to condemn him; see the judicious survey of the matter by S. Wessel, *Cyril of Alexandria and the Nestorian Controversy: The Making of a Saint and a Heretic* (Oxford: Oxford University Press, 2004), pp. 46–57. McGuckin gives a sympathetic discussion of Cyril's Christology, as do other modern authors. However, the problem seems to remain that, though Cyril declared that Christ was fully human in soul as well as in body, the human soul appears to be relatively passive in comparison with the divine soul. There is also the problem of whether, and how, Divinity can suffer. Despite Cyril's best efforts to explain this, one is left with the impression that Christ's soul had no more than a 'fellow feeling' with the agonies of its body on the Cross, or be more than 'impassibly aware of its flesh's sufferings'; H. Chadwick, 'Eucharist and Christology in the Nestorian Controversy' in *Journal of Ecclesiastical History* 2 (1951), p. 159.

Diet: a balanced diet. The whole matter of a balanced diet has been carefully considered by J. K. Evans, 'Plebs rustica II', *American Journal of Ancient History* 5 (1980), pp. 151–4, who has calculated a hypothetical diet for a moderately active adult male working in the Roman countryside. Calories come mainly from wheat, wine, olives, cheese, eggs and walnuts (in descending order of importance); proteins from wheat, eggs and cheese; vitamin A from carrots, parsley and eggs; and other significant contributions are made by figs, cabbage, radishes and garlic. Turnips, honey and almonds add significantly to the intake of calories or calcium. It is clear that Benedict's monks could not have remained fit and active without spreading their diet beyond the basic ingredients mentioned in *RB* 38. See also K. D. White, 'Food requirements and food supplies in Classical times in relation to the diet of the various classes' in *Progress in Food and Nutrition Science* 2 (1976), pp. 143–91. Two excellent general studies of food in Roman times are P. Garnsey, *Food and Society in Classical Antiquity* (Cambridge: Cambridge University Press, 1999) and A. Dalby, *Food in the Ancient World from A–Z* (London: Routledge, 2003).

Dionysius Exiguus. Only scraps of information about 'Denis the Little' now exist. He was probably born about 470 in Scythia (a region on the Black Sea coast, now Romania) and then spent some time in Constantinople, where he received his education and was professed as a monk. He was so fluent in Greek and Latin that he could read from one into the other on sight. He was recruited by Pope Gelasius to gather together and codify the canons passed by Church councils in East and West, but he seems not to have arrived in Rome until just after Gelasius's death in 496. His legal and archival work was extremely thorough and played an important part in bringing Church law together into a single corpus. After fulfilling Gelasius's commission, he went on to make collections of papal correspondence and then to work for Popes Hormisdas and John, but not, it seems (and this may be significant), for Symmachus.

Dionysius had a strong interest in the theology of the Eastern Church in general and of Alexandria in particular; he translated many Eastern theological works into Latin and worked for reconciliation between the two branches of the Church during the bitter disputes of the late fifth and early sixth centuries. He revised the system for computing the date of Easter, which was accepted by the whole Church in 532, and his calculations also provided a fixed date for the birth of Jesus according to the old Roman system, which facilitated the transition from dating *ab urbe condita* (that is, from the foundation of Rome) to the universally accepted system of BC/AD, now BCE/CE.

***Dominus, paterfamilias* and abbot**. Both Kardong (*Benedict's Rule*, p. 66) and *RB 1980*, pp. 353–4 are adamant that Benedict's discussion of the abbot is drawn from scriptural sources and monastic tradition and not from contemporary culture. Their view concentrates on the *paterfamilias* and overlooks the significance of the *dominus*. In any case, the household, led by a *paterfamilias*, continued to be a model for ecclesiastical organisation in the sixth century; Justinian (N. 81.3) required anyone elected bishop to become a *paterfamilias* even if his father or grandfather was still alive (he would normally have had to wait until the senior male of the family had died before taking the title himself); see Sessa, *Formation*, pp. 45–6. *RB 1980* and others fail to take account of the way that 'profane' writing on household leadership had increasingly emphasised its Christian virtues. These commentators are not able to be consistent in denying contemporary influences; for example, *RB 1980*, when discussing the abbot's role as an administrator, concedes that the parallel with the *paterfamilias* has 'a certain validity' (p. 369).

There are many studies of the Roman family, including R. P. Saller, *Patriarchy, Property and Death in the Roman Family* (Cambridge: Cambridge University Press, 1994) and K. Cooper, *The Fall of the Roman Household* (Cambridge: Cambridge University Press, 2007). See also O. Norderval, 'The Benedictine transformation of Roman villa life' in *Acta ad Archaeologiam et Artium Historiam Pertinenta* 16 (2002), pp. 31–8.

East and West. Throughout this book I use 'East' and 'West' as convenient shorthand terms for the two main divisions of the empire and the Church. By 'East' I am referring to the eastern provinces of the empire that stretched in an arc around the Mediterranean from the Balkans to Egypt. Their capital, Constantinople, was known locally as Byzantion, a name that was later applied to the whole region. The 'West' once embraced all the Roman provinces in western Europe and North Africa, but by the late fifth century only Italy remained. The Church can be divided in a similar way. The diocesan hierarchy of the whole of western Europe and north Africa was directly responsible to the pope, despite changes of government and periods of persecution. In the East the provinces of the Church were divided between the patriarchs of Constantinople, Antioch, Jerusalem and Alexandria. The patriarchs were prepared to concede the supremacy of the pope—though they did this rather grudgingly—but they preferred to see Church councils as the source of ultimate authority.

Farm management. My portrait of the *vilicus* (p. 96) draws on Columella, *On Agriculture* (*Res Rustica*) (Cambridge, MA: Harvard University Press, 2014) xi, 1, 18 and 19. Columella, who lived in the first century AD, was one of the leading Roman writers on rural affairs. The roles of *vilicus* and other managers were discussed by many other people over the centuries; for example, Cicero had said that a good ruler would be a combination of *dispensator* and *vilicus*, because the *dispensator* brought book-learning and the *vilicus* practical experience and both had so internalised their knowledge that it flowed naturally into all their practical activities. Cicero, *On the Commonwealth*, V, 5, trans./ed. J. E. G. Zetzel (Cambridge: Cambridge University Press, 1999), pp. 88–9.

The *vilicus* had a female companion, a *vilica*. She might be his wife, but it was equally common for her to be married to one of the other slaves. Her job was to clean and cook, look after the hens and the orchard and take care of the slaves' clothing. She was supposed to have high moral standards and not be greedy, gossipy or superstitious. Columella added that she ought to be young and pretty, though not enough to distract the *vilicus* from his work.

The Master thought that an abbot should avoid the distractions of estate management and rent out the monastery's lands to 'a secular lessee' (*Rule of the Master*, 86.1). The contradiction between this and Benedict's involvement in management is probably less that it seems; Benedict undoubtedly left the bulk of such work to his *dispensator* and *vilicus*. Even so, it is unlikely that the abbot of a newly established monastery such

Saint Benedict in his Community

as Monte Cassino would not have taken a personal interest in settling the management of newly donated land. The Master also thought that monks should avoid heavy agricultural work and confine themselves to handicrafts and light gardening (*ibid.*, 86.27), but it is very clear that Benedict expected his monks to work in the fields as well.

Food production and preservation: handbooks. When Cassiodorus founded his monastery at Squillace in the 550s he equipped it with copies of books by Palladius and Columella to help the monks grow their own food. Palladius's book *The Work of Farming* (*opus agriculturae*), which probably dates from 350–400, was an ideal beginners' guide, as it was organised chronologically into 'jobs for the month' and gave special tips on particular crops. Columella went into great detail on aspects of food preservation. For a fascinating modern discussion of this subject see D. L. Thurmond, *A Handbook of Food Processing in Classical Rome: For her Bounty no Winter* (Leiden: Brill, 2006).

The Gothic kings of those times. After Theoderic's death the sequence of leaders was as follows: Athalaric (r. 526–34) died after a bout of debauchery with his Gothic mates. His mother Amalasuntha (526–35) continued to rule and invited Theoderic's nephew Theodahad to take the throne alongside her, but he betrayed her and had her murdered. Theodahad (535–6) was deposed by Gothic military leaders who were exasperated by his feeble resistance to the imperial invaders; he was then murdered by his successor, Witigis (536–40), who presided over the retreat to the north and the abortive peace of 540, after which he surrendered and was taken to Constantinople. The Goths then chose Ildebad (540–1) and Eraric (541), but both fell out with one Gothic faction or another and Eraric was deposed when he was caught trying to negotiate another surrender in exchange for money. He was succeeded by Totila (541–52); see **Totila**, below. Teias (552–3) escaped from the debacle of Totila's final battle and was made king. He hoped to make an alliance with the Franks in exchange for money, but was intercepted and killed on his way to the Gothic treasury at Cumae.

Gregory the Great. Pope Gregory I was born in Rome in about 540 and grew up during the chaos of the Gothic War and the Lombard invasions. He came from an aristocratic family that was used to prominent roles in Church and state; his grandfather was Pope Felix III (483–92), his father was a senator and Gregory himself was elected Prefect of Rome in 573. In 575 he decided to become a monk and turned the family mansion in Rome into a monastery. In 579 Pope Pelagius II made him a deacon and sent him as papal ambassador to Constantinople, where he remained for seven years. He then returned to Rome and a life of prayer and philosophical reflection. In 590, to his dismay, he was elected pope. Much of his pontificate was taken up with worldly matters; in the absence of an effective government he had to manage the city's food supplies, respond to an epidemic of plague, and negotiate with Lombard warlords who constantly threatened to invade the city. He also carried through many reforms of the Church and produced several important books on ethics and pastoral care, as well as the *Dialogues*. He died in 604.

Gregory, *Dialogue*: factual evidence in the *Dialogue*. The factual evidence in the *Dialogue* is almost entirely discounted by de Vogüé, *Life*, Cusack, *An Interpretation of the Second Dialogue*, and J. M. Petersen, *The Dialogues of Gregory the Great in the Late Antique Cultural Background* (Toronto: Pontifical Institute of Medieval Studies, 1984). They have chosen to see the *Dialogue* as fabricated out of existing literary models, with scant regard for literal truth. I prefer to approach the *Dialogue* from the opposite direction. I believe that many of the stories have their origin in actual events, though Gregory has embellished them for moral effect and to create parallels with exsiting Christian literature. Clark, *'Gregorian' Dialogues*, pp. 127–8, argues that the *Dialogues* do not reflect the Italy of Gregory's time (the 590s), but in the case of *Dialogue* 2, it is the Italy of Benedict's time (500–50) which should provide the background—and it does.

Saint Benedict in his Community

The miracles recorded in the *Dialogue* may not be a representative sample of Benedict's activities; they may just be the events best remembered by the monks who had taken refuge in Rome and from which Gregory made selections to demonstrate Benedict's holiness. Benedict appears to have used his special power to provide the community with water (*Dialogue* 5.2–3), grain (21.1–2) and olive oil (29.1), but there is a rational explanation for each of these episodes, as I have argued in my text. The attempt to create a garden on the edge of the Subiaco lake (*Dialogue* 6.1) is what one would expect of a community struggling for self-sufficiency. Benedict's various prophecies were really no more than educated guesses: Totila's life expectancy was obviously low (*Dialogue* 15.1) and there was a strong chance that Monte Cassino would be destroyed in the wars (*Dialogue* 17.1). (It is worth noting that Benedict did not prophecy that the monastery would be destroyed by the Lombards, as is often alleged. He said it would be destroyed by 'barbarians', which he almost certainly assumed would be Goths. It was Gregory who subsequently identified the 'barbarians' with Lombards). As for the destruction of Rome (*Dialogue* 15.3), it is very likely that Benedict had heard about the disasters that had overwhelmed cities in the East and thought that Rome might suffer the same fate.

Half of the episodes in the *Dialogue* concern monks, as individuals, as a community, or as individuals out in the world. That is what one would expect. A notable feature is Benedict's insight into the characters of the individuals concerned, as in the case of the monk who accepted a gift of napkins (*Dialogue* 19.1–2) or the monk who held a lamp while Benedict ate (*Dialogue* 20.1–2). The same attention to detail is shown in episodes involving outsiders. Benedict's skill in dealing with these must have owed much to his upbringing in the household of a *curial* in Nursia and his experience as a holy man in Subiaco. Indebtedness is always a problem in peasant societies and it would have been made worse in sixth-century Italy by war and adverse weather. The difficulties between

Zalla and his tenant (*Dialogue* 31.1–4) were resolved by a face-to-face meeting with Benedict as broker; the case of the pious Christian who had fallen into debt (*Dialogue* 27.1–2) obviously took longer and may have involved helping the man to budget more efficiently. In the case of the two abusive nuns (*Dialogue* 23.2–5) Benedict dealt firmly but compassionately with all the parties. He reprimanded the two abusers, helped their victim to confront the situation and found a way of releasing their maidservant from the psychological trauma of living in an atmosphere of domestic violence.

Gregory, *Dialogues*: authenticity. Scepticism about the *Dialogues* has been taken a stage further by Francis Clark, who thinks that the style and content of the *Dialogues* are so much at variance with Gregory's other works that the *Dialogues* must be a forgery. He attributes them instead to a Lateran official writing about fifty years later. Clark published his thesis as *The Pseudo-Gregorian Dialogues*, 2 vols (Leiden: Brill, 1987). This book provoked a storm of criticism and in 2003 Clark restated his ideas in a shorter work containing answers to his critics: *The 'Gregorian' Dialogues and the Origins of Benedictine Monasticism* (Leiden: Brill, 2003). Clark has written a useful summary of his thesis—which makes very few concessions to his critics—in 'Authenticity of the Gregorian Dialogues: the widening debate' in *Analectica Monastica* 8 (2004), pp. 641–56.

Clark's knowledge is formidable and the controversy surrounding his books has been a useful one, but I am inclined to think that his argument is forced and the evidence, on balance, is against him. In July 593 Gregory wrote to Bishop Maximian of Syracuse saying that 'brethren' in Rome had asked him to write an account of the holy men of Italy; would Maximian therefore send him any stories that he knew of the miracles they had performed. I think this letter should be taken at face value (Clark thinks it is a second forgery to reinforce the first). I think it is almost certain that similar—though not identical—letters were sent to other bishops all over Italy (since the *Dialogue* stories come from many scattered sources) but that the people who organised Gregory's correspondence after his death kept only the one to Maximian as an example. The miracle stories in the *Dialogues* are therefore the raw data collected by Gregory's research and part of the rawness comes from the stories' diverse origins. In more than half of the cases Gregory names his informant. Clark thinks this is another ruse to convey 'verisimilitude', but I think that in doing so a forger would have created too many hostages to denial; if the informants themselves had died, there would still have been young relatives or assistants who would have been able to say whether or not the informants were in a position to know if the stories were true. In the case of *Dialogue* 2 the informants would have been the surviving members of Benedict's community, who had fled from Monte Cassino to Rome when the Lombards destroyed the monastery in the 570s, and were then living only a stone's throw from Gregory and were available for interview and consultation on points of detail. Because of this, Benedict receives a biographical treatment that cannot be attempted for the other characters in the *Dialogues*. The letters to Maximian and the other bishops mark only the start of Gregory's research into the holy men of Italy, research that was bound to take months if not years. While Clark is probably right in saying that Gregory was too busy with urgent political matters to write another book in 593–4, he is probably wrong in assuming that the projected book would have been written in those two years rather than spread over many years subsequently.

Gregory's aim was to write an account of Italian holy men that would equal the tales of the holy men of Gaul, such as St Martin of Tours. He also wanted to make sure that the activities of holy men were understood in a properly Christian way. Gregory was much concerned about the survival of paganism in late sixth-century Italy—indeed, he wrote another letter to Maximian on precisely that topic—and it was important that tales of holy men and their miracles were not left open to wild

Gregory, Dialogues: authenticity

pagan interpretations but were 'domesticated' by being told in a way that emphasised biblical parallels and canonical authority.

Clark's most fundamental objection to the *Dialogues* is this emphasis on miracles, many of which seem too ridiculous to be believed by anyone, then or now. Gregory was not credulous but—like many of the other leading thinkers of Late Antiquity, such as Augustine—he believed that miracles were a reminder of God's mysterious power beyond the natural order, as it was then understood. Gregory thought miracles were necessary to bring people to the faith and to show that God was still willing to intervene on behalf of his people in a world that was full of danger and confusion. This aspect of Gregory's thought has been examined by, among others, W. McCready, *Signs of Sanctity: Miracles in the Thought of Gregory the Great* (Toronto: Pontifical Institute of Medieval Studies, 1989) and M. dal Santo, 'The shadow of a doubt? A note on the Dialogues and Registrum Epistolarum of Gregory the Great (590–604)' in *Journal of Ecclesiastical History* 61 (2010), pp. 3–17.

Miracles are less of a problem in *Dialogue 2*, the life of Saint Benedict. To the modern reader, the stories it tells may seem a little quaint, but they are not necessarily irrational and in some cases not even miraculous. For example, several of the episodes tell us of Benedict's clairvoyance, but if it was possible to know every detail of the circumstances in which these insights occurred and to look into the faces of the other people involved, as Benedict was able to do, Benedict's conclusions would probably have seemed natural and understandable—perceptive, yes, but hardly miracles. I don't think the stories about Benedict are literally true in every detail, but I do think they have a substantial core of truth, albeit one that is coloured by parallels from scripture and ancient literature and an over-riding emphasis on Benedict's holiness.

Gregory worked on his books intermittently, writing when he had time and sending the manuscript back to the archives when he was otherwise engaged. It is possible, therefore, that the *Dialogues* as we know them are not the finished work that

Saint Benedict in his Community

Gregory intended. One scholar who has examined the abrupt and disjointed use of words in the *Dialogues* has suggested that they represent 'a stage in Gregorian composition when the author only tried to get a sequence of thoughts down in the barest prose', expecting to polish and refine them later. (This suggestion was made by Francis Newton in a letter to Paul Meyvaert, quoted in the latter's 'A comment on Francis Clark's response' in *Journal of Ecclesiastical History* 40 (1989), p. 345.) Other critics of Clark have also wondered if the *Dialogues* were work in progress, left unfinished at Gregory's death. This would help to account for the uneven quality of the *Dialogues*; the biography of Benedict seems a fairly finished piece of work, perhaps because the vivid reminiscences of the monks made it easy to write, whereas in *Dialogue 3* Gregory may still have been searching for interpretive threads with which to tie up that ragbag of miracle stories. If the *Dialogues* were unfinished at Gregory's death in 604 this would help to account for the delay in 'publication'—a somewhat elastic concept in those days—and the fact that the *Dialogues* do not seem to have been widely known until many years later.

The slow diffusion of the *Dialogues* and Benedict's *Rule* is, on the face of it, rather puzzling. Clark raises pertinent questions when he asks why, if the existence of the *Rule* and Benedict's saintly qualities had been advertised in *Dialogue 2*, it took so long for the *Rule* to be widely adopted and for the Church to accord Benedict the recognition he deserved. Gregory had known about the *Rule* but did not encourage its use in Italian monasteries and the first certain reference to its use appears to come from the diocese of Albi in Gaul in the 620s. In the middle decades of the seventh century many other monasteries in Gaul adopted it, but always in combination with the *Rule* of the Irish monk Columbanus. It was not until the very end of the century that Benedict's *Rule* was used in Rome. Clark thinks that the *Dialogues* were written in the second half of the seventh century to satisfy people's curiosity about the *Rule's* author. There is, on the other hand, some evidence that the *Dialogues* were known in Spain in the 630s and in 672 the monastery at Fleury in France—one of those that followed a combination of the Benedictine and Columbanian *Rules*—was sufficiently impressed by what it knew about Benedict, whether from *Dialogue 2* or some other source, to send a raiding party of monks to the ruins of Monte Cassino to dig up some of Benedict's bones and bring them back as holy relics. Benedict's incorporation into an official calendar of the Church's saints began early in the eighth century.

When considering this delay in the veneration of Benedict it is important not to be swayed by hindsight. In the early seventh century there were many monastic rules in circulation, notably that of Columbanus, who had travelled from Ireland to Gaul, Burgundy and ultimately to northern Italy, founding monasteries and introducing an Irish style of monasticism. It is not at all surprising that Benedict's *Rule* made slow headway against this competition. There may also have been some resistance from the Church establishment to acknowledge Benedict's personal qualities. There was tension between monks and secular clergy in the late sixth and early seventh centuries and Gregory had made himself very unpopular by promoting monks ahead of secular clergy. In this climate of opinion, reminders of Benedict may not have been welcome; he was, after all, only a layman, a layman who had been uncomfortably independent in his activities and rather too successful in his religious experiments. Benedict may have been regarded by the Church establishment with a mixture of irritation and jealousy and it may have been several decades before prejudice against him subsided and his contributions to the Christian life became appreciated.

Hymns from the fifth century. In his liturgical code Benedict asks for 'an Ambrosian hymn' to be sung at Vigils (*RB* 9.4), at Lauds (*RB* 13.11) and at Vespers (*RB* 17.8). St Ambrose, bishop of Milan in 375–97, was one of the pioneers of hymn composition. His hymns were written in verses of four short lines with regular verbal rhythms which were easy to memorise.

Saint Benedict in his Community

Ambrose also wrote many of the tunes. The hymns were interspersed through long sequences of psalms and were intended to emphasise essential points of doctrine and to praise God through the hours of the day. Not all the hymns that bear Ambrose's name are certainly his, but one that is clearly authentic is *Deus Creator omnium*, which begins in translation: 'Creator of the earth and sky/ Ruling the firmament on high'. Benedict is using 'Ambrosian hymn' as a category, rather than as hymns specifically by Ambrose (indeed, he omits a word for hymn and simply says *ambrosianum*; Parry, *Rule*, simply says 'hymn'). It must therefore be a possibility that hymns by Prudentius and others were also sung in the monastery. Some of Prudentius's hymns survive in modern hymnals, such as his poem on the Holy Innocents: *Salvete flores martyrum*, 'All hail, ye little martyr flowers / sweet rosebuds cut in dawning hours'. Benedict would almost certainly have known a Christmas hymn by Sedulius: *A solis ortus cardine*,'From east to west, from shore to shore / Let every heart awake and sing'. See C. White, *Early Christian Latin Poets* (New York: Routledge, 2000). J. A. McGuckin, *The Path of Christianity: The First Thousand Years* (Downers Grove, IL: IVP Press, 2017), pp. 845–8, has translations of two of Ambrose's hymns with a discussion of their theological content.

Justinian was born Petrus Sabbatius in about 482, the son of a peasant family in what is now south-east Serbia. He went to Constantinople to join the imperial guard which was led by his uncle Justin. In 518 Justin became emperor, but his nephew, now known as Justinian, was always the power behind the throne and was the natural successor when Justin died in 527. Justinian is rightly celebrated for initiating and overseeing a project to codify the whole of Roman law, a code that bears his name and was the foundation of European law for the next millennium.

Justinian's foreign policy had less happy outcomes. He never came to terms with the rising power of Persia on his eastern border and war continued intermittently throughout his reign.

Libraries

His great ambition was to reunite the territories of the old Roman empire in the western Mediterranean. He achieved a quick victory over the Vandal kingdom of North Africa in 533–4 and this emboldened him to attack the Ostrogoths in Italy, a campaign that became a military quagmire and an economic disaster. In the early 550s he sent an expeditionary force against the Visigoths of Spain, with only slight success.

In domestic policy Justinian was assisted by very effective ministers and, in a couple of moments of real crisis, by his formidable wife Theodora. He kept control of religious policy as he considered himself something of an expert in those matters. He took his duties seriously, lived rather austerely, seldom travelled, worked enormously long hours and had an eye for detail. Though he could be utterly ruthless in crushing opposition, he was affable and approachable on a personal level, genuinely distressed by the suffering of his subjects in plagues and earthquakes and a generous donor to schemes for their relief. He died in 565.

Libraries. There were 28 public libraries in Rome in the late fourth century, according to one source, and it is likely that many of these survived into the sixth century. Libraries were incorporated into the imperial bathing complexes and also built close to temples. The library in the Baths of Caracalla consisted of two halls of about 36 m x 22 m, with a colonnaded screen separating them from the ambulatory outside, which is probably where most of the reading was done because the light was better. The book storage was on two floors with ladders to the upper level. The Bibliotheca Ulpia originally had enough storage space for 40,000 scrolls, though this would have been converted later into shelving for a smaller number of books. Access to libraries was free but was, obviously, restricted in practice to the minority who could read. The book stock probably focused on law and literature and was intended as a window on to classical culture, not to entertain or educate the mass of the people. See F. Yegul, *Baths and Bathing in Classical Antiquity* (Cambridge, MA: Harvard University Press, 1992).

Saint Benedict in his Community

Private libraries had seats and desks and a variable amount of book storage along the walls. For some householders, the library was a place for serious study where they could follow their literary and philosophical interests (as evidently happened in a library unearthed at Pompeii); for others, it was a fashionable place to chat with friends, where books in fine bindings sat unread upon the shelves.

The local churches of Rome had congregational archives and libraries covering a wide range of material: biblical commentaries, controversial tracts, reports from Church synods and accounts of the lives of saints and the deaths of martyrs, some of them very colourful and corrupted by pagan traditions of magic and visions. These libraries seem to have been collected and catalogued systematically for scholarly purposes. Jerome advised a correspondent who was puzzled on a theological point to wait until he got to Rome and then seek an answer in the libraries there. Christians were very conscious of the literary tradition that reinforced their faith. The library of Pope Agapitus, which was similar to the libraries in the bathing complexes in scale and design, contained an inscription as follows: 'A venerable company of saints sits in a long line / teaching the mystical precepts of divine law / the priest Agapitus is appropriately seated among them / he has built with art this beautiful place for books'. Benedict was also conscious of this tradition (*RB* 73.4). See H. Y. Gamble, *Books and Readers in the Early Church: A History of Early Christian Texts* (New Haven: Yale University Press, 1995) who quotes the inscription about Agapitus on p. 165 and M. H. Williams, *The Monk and the Book: Jerome and the Making of Christian Scholarship* (Chicago: Chicago University Press, 2006).

Libraries/*Bibliotheca*. The restricted use of *bibliotheca* was proposed by A. Mundó in an influential article: '"Bibliotheca", Bible et lecture du carême d'apres Saint Benoit' in *Revue bénédictine* 60 (1950), pp. 65–92. Mundó assembled two lists of early Christian authors: those who used *bibliotheca* in the normal

Manichaeism

sense—a repository of books—and those who used it as a synonym for the Bible. The weakness in Mundó's thesis is that more than half of the authors in his second list come from the period after Benedict's death and from circumstances very different from Benedict's; indeed, Mundó himself admits that this use of *bibliotheca* became more fashionable in the Middle Ages. The two authors who lived in the same decades as Benedict and came from the same cultural background—Boethius and Cassiodorus—both used *bibliotheca* to mean a book repository. An extreme version of the Mundó thesis has been offered by A. Petrucci, *Writers and Readers in Medieval Italy: Studies in the History of a Written Culture* (New Haven: Yale University Press, 1995), p. 34, who seems to imagine Benedict as some kind of anti-intellectual zealot. Part of his argument is a mis-reading of *RB* 33.3, where Benedict says that a monk shall not retain as his own any book, writing tablet or stylus. Petrucci seems to believe that Benedict was trying to stamp out the use of these articles, but, in fact, Benedict was not denouncing books and styluses as such, but the creeping privatisation of monastic property and he gives these items as examples precisely because everyone needed to use them.

Manichaeism is the teaching of Mani (216–74), a preacher who lived in Persia but whose ideas spread widely, from Spain, North Africa and Rome to the borders of China. Mani argued that the cosmos was in the grip of a struggle between Light and Darkness. He saw Jesus as a cosmic principle operating through various entities to release Light from Darkness, but none of these manifestations can be equated with the historical Jesus of Nazareth. Because Darkness was inherent in materiality, he advocated rigorous asceticism. Saint Augustine was a follower of Mani for some years as a young man.

Meat eating. St Paul said that no food was 'unclean in itself' (Rom 14:14), but Cassian, Jerome and others condemned all meat-eating because it was believed to increase the heat of the body and lead to lust. See D. M. Bazell, 'Strife among

Saint Benedict in his Community

the table-fellows: conflicting attitudes of early and medieval Christians towards the eating of meat' in *Journal of the American Academy of Religion* 65 (1997), pp. 73–99, and A. Böckmann, *Around the Monastic Table—RB 31–42: Growing in Mutual Service and Love* (Collegeville: Liturgical Press, 2009), pp. 163–4. Was a distinction made between red and white meat? Some, including the Master (*Rule of the Master* 53.27, 31–2) seem to have done so, but it is not clear if such a view was widespread in the early sixth century. Romans generally thought meat-eating a bit extravagant because animals—other than pigs—were expensive to rear and prepare for the table. Hens, on the other hand, cost nothing and were found everywhere in the countryside. It was therefore possible for monastic communities to eat chicken without offending any of their principles of ascesis.

Monks: the number of monks. According to the *Dialogue* (3.13), the Subiaco community was divided into twelve priories with twelve monks in each, together with a small household of novices living with Benedict himself—a total, let us say, of 150 monks. Because of its biblical significance, the number twelve needs to be treated with caution; on the other hand, Schuster, *Benedict*, pp. 81–3, says that there are local legends identifying twelve sites for these priories. It is possible that the number of monks in each priory might have been ten, by analogy with the Roman army, where the smallest unit contained ten men. It would not be unreasonable, therefore, to conclude that the Subiaco community was well over 100 strong, perhaps about 120–30. From these, Benedict took a contingent to Monte Cassino of, say, twenty—about the minimum needed to found a new community. The Monte Cassino community then grew to a maximum of 30–40; archaeological evidence suggests that the oratory could not have held many more than this. Another contingent of 20 then went to Terracina and were replaced by new recruits at Monte Cassino. Altogether the total number of monks living under Benedict's direction must have been 150 and perhaps more.

The Ostrogothic succession crisis

The Ostrogothic succession crisis. It has been suggested—very plausibly—that Theoderic's real concern was his inability to get everyone to agree on his successor. He had no son, so he arranged for his daughter Amalasuntha to marry Eutharic, a Visigothic prince from Spain. The couple quickly produced a son, Athalaric, and the succession seemed assured. What's more, it gave a dynastic dimension to the link between Italy and the territories in southern Gaul and northern Spain that Theoderic had recently absorbed into his kingdom (see **Theoderic**, below). The imperial court in Constantinople approved this plan for the succession, perhaps because Justin and his nephew didn't feel strong enough to oppose Theoderic at this stage and perhaps because Theoderic had been helpful in settling a long-running theological dispute between the pope and the patriarch of Constantinople. Unfortunately Eutharic died in 522–3. Theoderic now had to seek imperial approval all over again, this time for Athalaric. This time Justin and Justinian were not inclined to be accommodating, especially as Theoderic had nothing to offer in return. Indeed, Theoderic's position had suddenly become much weaker as the Burgundian and Vandal regimes began to manoeuvre against the aging king in the hope of getting back their lost territories. Factions opposed to Amalasuntha began to form in Ravenna and Justinian seized this moment to begin his campaign against the Arian churches in Constantinople.

It is possible that Boethius got mixed up in this plotting and backed the wrong faction. The most obvious alternative to Amalasuntha was Theoderic's nephew Theodahad, who was said to have been a bit of a scholar and might have seemed to Boethius to be the philosopher-king that he yearned to see on the throne. Not only that, but Boethius, who had good contacts in Constantinople, was conspicuously failing to use them on Amalasuntha's behalf. On both counts, therefore, Theoderic might have considered him treacherous. His fall from power did not reflect upon the Catholic senatorial elite as a whole, since other members of the elite replaced him.

Perfume making. The whole process is depicted in a wall-painting in Pompeii, which shows the pressing of oil at one end and, at the other, an elegant lady sniffing samples of perfume from the back of her hand. See D. J. Mattingly, 'Painting, presses and perfume production at Pompeii' in *Oxford Journal of Archaeology* 9 (1990), pp. 33–56. The evidence about markets comes from plaques inscribed with the names of market towns in Campania (including Casinum and Aquinum) and the days of the month. Peg-holes alongside each name made it possible for a merchant to remind himself of the next market day in each town and plot his route accordingly. See R. MacMullen, 'Market-days in the Roman empire' in *Phoenix* 24 (1970), pp. 333–41. When the demand for perfumes fell as a result of the emigration of aristocratic families to Constantinople, the monastery would have been in a good position to supply the Church's rising demand for aromatic oils.

Plague: diagnosing the plague. There are descriptions of the symptoms and progress of the plague from contemporary authors (the most clinical is by Procopius, who caught the infection himself but survived; see his *Wars*, 2.22.10–39). The majority of victims had buboes in the groin and the armpits and on the neck. In cases where bacilli had infected the lungs, the disease was spread by inhalation; and if septicaemia occurred, there could be sudden death from heart failure. Other common symptoms were hallucinations and coma. Some modern authors have resisted the plague diagnosis, but the case for it has been argued convincingly by R. Sallares, 'Ecology, evolution and epidemiology of plague' in L. K. Little, ed., *Plague and the End of Antiquity: The Pandemic of 541–750* (Cambridge: Cambridge University Press, 2007), pp. 231–89. The pandemic is set in a wider context by K. Harper, *The Fate of Rome: Climate, Disease and the End of an Empire* (Princeton University Press, 2017).

The plague bacillus appears to have been endemic among the various wild rodents of central Africa and, at some point, they may have moved northwards into Egypt, where their

The popes of those times

territory overlapped with that of the black rat and its flea, which picked up the bacillus and transferred it to humans. The spread of the disease was patchy and jerky, from town to town and from street to street, depending on the movement of rats. The pneumonic form of the disease spread more easily through the inhalation of droplets of vapour from an infected person and plague could travel like wildfire through places where people worked and slept alongside each other. This may have been the form of plague that swept through Constantinople in 542.

How did Benedict and his community escape? The second European pandemic of plague, the Black Death of 1348–51, was a catastrophe for the Benedictine Order, reducing many monasteries to just a handful of members. If the same fate had overtaken Monte Cassino we might never have heard of Benedict or his *Rule*. The community was probably saved by its relative isolation, both physical and social, and especially its isolation from the black rat. Left to themselves, rats do not travel far—their territory does not usually have a radius of more than 200 metres—but they like hitching rides on boats and carts. For this reason rat infestation in Roman Italy is usually associated with a coastal port, a riverside town or a paved road. Rats do not like to ride on pack animals, which were the only way of carrying supplies to the summit of Monte Cassino. Though an infected flea might have made the journey up the mountain in a bundle on a mule, the reluctance of the rats to make the same journey may have limited the risk of infection and saved the monks' lives. The movement of rats is discussed in M. McCormick, 'Rats, communication and plague: toward an ecological history' in *Journal of Interdisciplinary History* 34 (2003), pp. 1–25.

The popes of those times. The popes who held office in Benedict's lifetime were as follows: Felix III (483–92), a Roman of aristocratic background, was succeeded by the man who had been the power behind his throne, the formidable Gelasius (492–6), who was of African descent. Gelasius gave an impression of arrogance and rigidity but as a person was said to have

Saint Benedict in his Community

been humble, devoted to his work and generous to the poor. Anastasius II (496–8) was followed by a contested election and a long schism (see my Chapter 6) between Laurentius (498–506) and the eventual winner Symmachus (498–514). Hormisdas (514–23), despite his Persian name, was from a town in Latium, not far from Rome. He settled the serious theological conflict between Rome and Constantinople. The pontificate of John I (523–6) was followed by several bitterly contested elections in which Felix IV (526–30) had the balance tipped in his favour by Theoderic; Boniface II (530–2), the favourite of the Gothic court, was accepted reluctantly by the Roman clergy when his opponent, Dioscorus, who had been enthroned in a separate ceremony on the same day, died within two months; the saintly John II (532–5), a priest at one of the Roman churches, emerged as a compromise when the main candidates ran out of money to pay bribes; after which the factions were too exhausted to fight over Agapitus (535–6), who was elected in six days. Silverius (536–7), an obscure sub-deacon, was propelled into office by Theodahad, who was determined to have a friend in the Lateran when Justinian's invasion began. Silverius soon found himself in a Rome under siege and in theological conflict with the patriarch of Constantinople. He was deposed by Theodora and Belisarius in favour of Vigilius (537–55).

Proba. Faltonia Betitia Proba was probably born *c.* 320 and died *c.* 370. Her names suggest a senatorial background and she may have been the daughter of the man who was consul in 322 and later the wife of the governor of Apulia and Calabria. She probably wrote the cento in the last decade or so of her life. Her poem retained its popularity throughout the Middle Ages and was usually found in the 'educational' section of monastic libraries. She was the most widely read female author before modern times. There is a translation of the cento in E. A. Clark and D. F. Hatch, *The Golden Bough, the Oaken Cross: The Virgilian Cento of Faltonia Betitia Proba* (Chico: Scholars Press, 1981). That the cento was one of the 'apocryphal scriptures' was the judgement of Isidore of Seville (570–636).

Procopius

Procopius was a Palestinian, born in Caesarea in about 500. He had a conventional legal career before being appointed to Belisarius's staff as a legal secretary. He accompanied Belisarius on his campaign against the Vandals in 533, and then against the Ostrogoths from 536 until at least 540. Procopius was in Constantinople in 542, where he witnessed the epidemic of plague. It is not clear whether he rejoined Belisarius in Italy later in the 540s, but if he did not, he would still have had contacts in the army who fed him information. His account of the second part of the Italian campaign has fewer dramatic battle scenes and is more concerned about the general direction of the war as he began to realise what a disaster it had become and his sympathies became more evenly distributed between the imperial cause and the Goths. Procopius's ambition was to be a great military historian in the manner of Thucydides and some of his scenes are modelled on equivalent episodes in the latter's *Peloponnesian War*. Procopius is therefore guilty of some distortion for literary effect but the facts he provides are thought to be fairly accurate.

In addition to the *Wars*, Procopius wrote a book about Justinian's public buildings, which takes a very favourable view of the emperor, and the *Anekdota* (usually translated as *The Secret History*), which was a bitter attack on the imperial couple and their policies. The many differences between these books have been discussed by A. Kaldellis, *Procopius of Caesarea: Tyranny, History and Philosophy at the End of Antiquity* (Philadelphia: University of Pennsylvania Press, 2004).

Purple. The purple made in Aquinum should not be confused with the intense purple used for royal robes and regalia and for the decorative borders on the togas of senators and other members of the elite. That colour was made from the secretion of a gland in a particular type of shellfish, a process that was very time-consuming and expensive. Cheap imitations made from vegetable dye were widely available; for example, in Gaul a dark purple dye made from whortleberry was used for slaves' clothes because it hid the dirt. The black habits that

Saint Benedict in his Community

later became a defining characteristic of Benedictine monks were introduced as part of the standardisation of the Order which began in the ninth century.

The Roman emperors of those times were not successive generations of an imperial family and none of them ever visited Rome. Zeno (474–91) was a warlord from the mountains of Isauria (southern Turkey), who moved to Constantinople as an ally of the Emperor Leo I (457–74), married his daughter and fathered his heir, Leo II (474). When the two Leos died in quick succession, Zeno claimed the throne but immediately lost it to a usurper. It took two years of murder and manoeuvre to get it back. Anastasius I (491–518) came from Dyrrachion (a coastal town in what is now Albania). He was one of an elite group of bureaucrats who carried out difficult and sensitive missions for the imperial government and, as such, caught the eye of Zeno's widow, Ariadne, who ensured his selection as emperor and then married him. Justin I (518–27) was a farmer's son from Bederiana (now in Serbia) who rose to be leader of the palace guard. On Anastasius's death the guard split into factions, each with a claimant to the throne, but Justin emerged as the candidate who rose above the deadlock between the rest. During his reign the real power was exercised by his nephew and eventual heir, Justinian (526–65); see **Justinian**, above.

Rome: a plan for its destruction. The second siege was almost certainly the context of the discussion which Benedict had with the Bishop of Canosa, reported by Gregory in the *Dialogue* (15.3). The two men had been sharing their sadness at the sufferings of Rome and the bishop wondered if the Goths would bring about the city's complete destruction. Benedict disagreed, possibly because he had already met Totila and was able to form some assessment of his character, or perhaps because he was more impressed by the forces of nature that had shaken the Mediterranean world in recent years. Rome would not be destroyed by human hands, he said, but by tempests, lightning and earthquakes.

Sant' Apollinare Nuovo mosaics

The bishop's pessimism may have been prompted by Totila's plan for the destruction of Rome. After he had captured the city, Totila summoned the surviving members of the senate to a meeting in which he upbraided them for forgetting the benefits they had received under Theoderic's rule and for bringing in 'the Greeks' to attack their own fatherland. Totila then decided to tear down the walls and historic centre of the city. Part of the wall was indeed reduced in height, but before he could do anything to the buildings Totila received a plea for clemency from, of all people, Belisarius. Belisarius pointed out that Rome had become such a monument to civilisation, art and beauty that to destroy it would be 'a great crime against the whole of humanity'. If Totila won the war, he would want the city as his capital. After receiving this letter, 'Totila read it over many times and, accurately understanding the significance of the advice', rescinded his order (Procopius, *Wars*, 7.22.8–17).

Sant' Apollinare Nuovo mosaics. The theological significance of these has been much debated. Above the north side of the nave a series of small panels depict the ministry and miracles of a youthful Christ; above the south side, an older and bearded Christ is shown in scenes from the Passion. The difference in Christ's appearance is thought to reflect the Arian emphasis on his humanity; 'he is youthful and clean-shaven when divine, but he is older, and bearded as a Palestinian might have been, when his human nature is being emphasized' (N. MacGregor and E. Langmuir, *Seeing Salvation: Images of Christ in Art* (London: BBC Worldwide, 2000), p. 81. A similar position has been taken by D. MacCulloch, *A History of Christianity: The First Three Thousand Years* (London: Allen Lane, 2009), p. 321. At the same time there are similarities between the two friezes in points of detail and bearded representations of Christ can be found in the mosaics of those Catholic churches in Ravenna which were being constructed at the same time as Sant' Apollinare Nuovo. Orthodox Christians asserted the 'full humanity' as well as the 'full divinity' of Jesus, a view of the Saviour which did not preclude the process of aging or the growing of a beard. For a

Saint Benedict in his Community

good overview of the whole question see A. Urbano, 'Donation, dedication and *damnatio memoriae*: the Catholic reconciliation of Ravenna and the church of Sant' Apollinare Nuovo' in *Journal of Early Christian Studies* 13 (2005), pp. 71–110. Others who are sceptical about the Arianism of the mosaics are R. M. Jensen, *Face to Face: The Portrait of the Divine in Early Christianity* (Minneapolis: Fortress, 2004), pp. 159–65; D. M. Deliyannis, *Ravenna in Late Antiquity* (Cambridge: Cambridge University Press, 2010), pp. 156–8; and B. Ward-Perkins, 'Where is the archaeology and iconography of Germanic Arianism?' in D. M. Gwynn and S. Bangert, eds, *Religious Diversity in Late Antiquity* (Leiden: Brill, 2010), pp. 265–89. There are interesting discussions of the mosaics on-line.

Semi-Pelagianism. The Scythian monks had drafted the 'Confession' in a way that broadened the terms of the debate. They realised that people who emphasised the distinct humanity of Christ, albeit a humanity infused with divinity, might see Christ primarily as a model to be emulated by our own efforts, whereas those who saw Christ as the Word made flesh would regard this as the supreme example of God's prevenient and continuing grace. This stirred the embers of an old controversy between Augustine and the teacher Pelagius, a spiritual guide to the Roman aristocracy between 390 and 410. Augustine insisted on the absolute priority of divine grace, whereas Pelagius emphasised the responsibility of individual Christians to obey the moral code set forth in Scripture. The dispute was settled in 418 by an imperial decree in Augustine's favour. However, monastic communities continued to be worried by the issue because, if individual responsibility was so much discounted, what was the point of their ascetic lifestyle? Cassian attempted to find a compromise. He was critical of Pelagius but thought that grace and free will could cooperate, with grace stimulating and supporting the will and, at times, bringing to fruition what arises 'from our own efforts' (*Conf.* 13.8.4). This last point was too much for Augustine's admirers in southern

Semi-Pelagianism

Gaul and Cassian was accused of a new heresy, which came to be known as semi-Pelagianism. The controversy flared up from time to time during the rest of the fifth century and again in the 520s. On that occasion bishop Caesarius of Arles proposed a new compromise, this time leaning more obviously towards Augustine. This formula was approved by the Council of Orange (Arausio, in south-eastern France) in 529. Caesarius was working, in part, from florilegia of Augustine which had been collected by the Scythian monks, sent to the pope, and forwarded by the pope to Caesarius. According to the Council, the proper exercise of the will 'can be restored only through the grace of baptism' (Canon 13); after that, Christians may believe that they 'perform their actions voluntarily, [but] what they do is actually the will of him who prepares and commands what they will' (Canon 23).

It is not known if Benedict knew about the decisions made at Orange. He says (Prol. 4) that 'whenever you begin any good work, you must ask God with the most urgent prayer that it may be brought to completion by him'—which would seem to be following Cassian in giving priority to free will. However, in the very next verse, Benedict reminds his monks that God 'has now deigned to reckon us in the number of his sons'. This picks up ideas of adopted son-ship which can be found in Cassian (*Conf.* 1.15.2 and 11.9.1–3) and which clearly imply the priority of grace. A modern commentator has put the matter in this way: 'In a sense, monastic life is simply a structured means of placing oneself permanently within the ambit of Christ's operation—allowing oneself to be acted upon, challenged, changed, transformed over the course of a lifetime' (M. Casey, *The Road to Eternal Life: Reflections on the Prologue of Benedict's Rule* (Collegeville: Liturgical Press, 2012), p. 24).

Kardong, *Benedict's Rule*, pp. 9–10, 30–1, has useful comments on Benedict's ideas. There is an extensive literature on semi-Pelagianism generally. See R. H. Weaver, *Divine Grace and Human Agency: A Study of the Semi-Pelagian Controversy* (Macon, GA: Mercer University Press, 1996); D. J. Mcqueen,

'John Cassian on grace and freewill, with particular reference to Institutio XII and Collatio XIII', *Recherches de théologie ancienne et medievale* 44 (1977), pp. 5–28; D. Fairbairn, *Grace and Christology in the Early Church* (Oxford: Oxford University Press, 2003); R. W. Mathisen, 'Caesarius of Arles, prevenient grace and the Second Council of Orange' in A. Y. Hwang,, B. Matz and A. Casiday, eds, *Grace for Grace: the Debates after Augustine and Pelagius* (Washington, DC: Catholic University of America Press, 2014), pp. 208–34; a translation of the canons of Orange is in J. P. Burns, *Theological Anthropology* (Philadelphia: Fortress Press, 1981, pp. 112–20).

Sexual mores and the papacy. The Roman aristocracy had become very embittered by the attitude of Gelasius towards the sexual misconduct of some members of the clergy. A Campanian estate owner had complained to the pope that a priest had abducted a woman from his estate and forced her into marriage, but Gelasius not only refused to admit the offence but threatened to excommunicate the landowner and report him to Theoderic if he persisted with the matter. Gelasius also refused to discipline a Roman priest who had been caught in adultery. He then tried to close down Rome's festival of Lupercalia, which the aristocracy had organised for generations past, calling it 'spiritual adultery'. It was true that in earlier centuries the Lupercalia had been bawdy and disgusting, but in more recent times its sexual licence had been replaced by satirical tableaux. Gelasius suspected—probably quite correctly—that he and the errant clergy were going to be the butt of the satire. It may be that in the fuss about Conditaria, some members of the elite were enjoying a bit of *schadenfreude* at finding the pope himself in a compromising position and Symmachus was therefore being made to suffer for the obduracy of his predecessor.

Sheep farming. There is no hint in either the *Rule* or the *Dialogue* that Benedict's community was involved in sheep farming, but there would have been significant advantages in doing so: sheep's cheese was an important part of the diet and sheepskin and wool were important commodities. The neighbouring town of Aquinum contained a fulling mill and dye factories, which suggests that this was a wool-producing area. Sheep were normally kept around the farmstead where they could be tended and milked by the workers' children and allowed to forage wherever their dung would enrich the ground. The work required a squad of shepherds and an overseer known as a *magister pecoris*, a head shepherd with a role similar to that of a *vilicus*. In the spring the *magister pecoris* would lead the flocks and their shepherds into the Abruzzi where they circulated along the ancient drovers' roads and grazed in the high summer pastures. Sheep farming was popular with monastic communities because as long as the *magister pecoris* was capable and trustworthy, there was little more for the community to do. See J. Frayn, *Sheep-Rearing and the Wool Trade in Italy during the Roman Period* (Liverpool: Liverpool University Press, 1984).

Slavery. For Paul's teaching see Eph 6:5–9, Col 3:23–4:1 and 1 Tim 6:1–2. For Gregory's views see A. Serfass, 'Slavery and Pope Gregory the Great' in *Journal of Early Christian Studies* 14 (2006), pp. 77–103. Justinian's law (N.5.2–3) reflects the attitude of the times; it is humane in tone, but shows no inclination to change the system. Most slaves were employed in domestic service. A senatorial family might have several dozen of them, a curial family perhaps ten or so, some of them responsible for household chores, others dressing hair, playing music at meals, doing secretarial work, or just trailing the mistress of the house round the city streets in a retinue. A lot of them were grossly under-employed and drifted into a life of dissipation to relieve the boredom; this was the reason for Columella's warning to landowners about recruiting *vilici* from urban slaves. There are some examples of slaves who entered monasteries but soon asked to go back to their masters because they found domestic slavery preferable to monastic austerity. Domestic slaves could develop relationships with members of the family

Saint Benedict in his Community

which led to conflicting emotions over time; for example, the child of a slave, who grew up alongside a child of the family and became used to treating it as a sibling, would suddenly find, at about the age of puberty, that the two of them were separated by an unbridgeable gulf of status. Slave women could become entangled in mother-in-law/daughter-in-law conflicts and get themselves beaten as a substitute for one side or the other. These aspects are skilfully analysed by P. Clark, 'Women, slaves and the hierarchies of domestic violence: the family of Augustine' in S. R. Joshel and S. Murnaghan, eds, *Women and Slaves in Greco-Roman Culture: Differential Equations* (London: Routledge, 1998), pp. 109–29. There is an extensive literature on the subject of slavery which includes S. R. Joshel, *Slavery in the Roman World* (Cambridge: Cambridge University Press, 2010); C. Grey, 'Slavery in the late Roman world', ch. 22 in *The Cambridge World History of Slavery*, v.1, *The Ancient Mediterranean World* (Cambridge: Cambridge University Press, 2011) and K. Bradley, *Slavery and Society at Rome* (Cambridge: Cambridge University Press, 1994).

Theoderic was born in 454, the son of the second of three brothers who had consolidated the power of the Amal family over the Ostrogoths of Pannonia. The Amals had been receiving subsidies from the imperial government to ensure their good behaviour and they had also been required to send a young family member to live at court in Constantinople as a kind of gilded hostage. This obligation fell upon Theoderic. He probably went to Constantinople when he was seven and stayed for ten years. At the very least he would have learned some court etiquette and diplomatic protocol, taken part in processions and watched spectacles in the hippodrome, but he may also have had some formal education; it was in the interests of the imperial authorities to turn their hostages into Roman gentlemen who spoke the same language, subscribed to Roman values and might therefore become allies at some point in the future. How much of this rubbed off on to Theoderic is

Theoderic

not entirely clear. His Latin may have been a little weak, but he was probably well educated in Greek and Gothic. His court in Ravenna became a congenial place for historians, philosophers and other writers and the historic buildings of the city show Theoderic's own good taste in art and architecture.

The identity of Theoderic's first wife is unknown; it is possible she was not a wife but a concubine. She gave birth to two daughters who married into royal houses at about the time that Theoderic was taking control in Italy, one to the king of the Burgundians, the other to the king of the Visigoths. In about 493 Theoderic married Audofleda, sister of the king of the Franks, and the couple produced a daughter, Amalasuntha, who briefly became ruler of Italy after Theoderic's death. Theoderic was a major player in the geopolitics of the western Mediterranean. He seized Sicily from the Vandal kingdom of North Africa (Sicily's wheat fields were an economically important prize) and in 504–5 he pushed the north-eastern border of Italy a hundred miles further into Dalmatia, despite military opposition from the emperor in Constantinople. In 508 he came to the aid of the Visigothic kingdom of Spain in its war with the Franks and the Burgundians and was rewarded with a strip of territory along the Mediterranean coast of Gaul all the way from the Italian border to the Pyrenees (what is now Languedoc and Provence). This became a Gothic prefecture, governed from Arles but with oversight from Ravenna.

The only certain likeness of Theoderic that remains shows him in an imperial pose with his hair piled on the top of his head and a small, well-trimmed moustache.

Information about Theoderic, with extensive bibliographies, can be found in P. J. Heather, *The Restoration of Rome: Barbarian Popes and Imperial Pretenders* (London: Pan Books, 2014); J. Moorhead, *Theoderic in Italy* (Oxford: Clarendon Press, 1992); J. J. Arnold, *Theoderic and the Roman Imperial Restoration* (New York: Cambridge University Press, 2014); and J. Herrin, *Ravenna: Capital of Empire, Crucible of Europe* (London: Allen Lane, 2020).

Saint Benedict in his Community

Theodora. Procopius (see **Procopius**, above) has written such an acerbic description of her in *The Secret History* that one's reaction is to gasp, laugh and then forget to exercise any critical judgement. There are modern translations of the *History*, for example by G. A. Williamson and P. Sarris (London: Penguin, 2007), which should be complemented by the careful assessment of the evidence about Theodora, both favourable and unfavourable, by historians such as C. Foss, 'The Empress Theodora' in *Byzantion* 72 (2002), pp. 141–76. Foss concludes that Procopius was guilty of exaggeration rather than invention and that much of what he says about Theodora is reasonably reliable.

It seems probable that Theodora was born about 490 to parents who worked in the circus at Constantinople. Theodora was put on the stage as soon as she reached puberty and her work probably included strip-shows and prostitution. She had one or two children before she was 30 and was the mistress of a number of high-ranking officials before she caught the eye of Justinian, who had to have special legislation passed in order to marry her, probably about 523 (people of senatorial rank were normally prevented from marrying actresses).

Justinian lavished money and landed estates on Theodora so that she was wealthy enough to run her own network of spies, jailers and assassins. She endowed a number of charities (the condition of women was a particular interest of hers) and she seems to have lived a life of genuine piety after her marriage. Although she was never formally the co-ruler of the empire, she played a significant role in supporting her husband — and occasionally working at odds with him, as in the case of her backing for the Monophysites in the great religious controversy of the times (though it may be that Justinian thought it was useful for the palace to be facing in both directions simultaneously on this issue). Theodora's influence on Italian affairs was considerable. She helped to organise the murder of the Gothic Queen Amalasuntha and she sent the papal representative in Constantinople, an ambitious deacon named Vigilius, back

Totila: Benedict's meeting with him

to Rome with an enormous bribe to get Belisarius to depose the incumbent pope, Silverius, and put Vigilius in his place. Silverius was sent into exile and starved to death. Theodora was vengeful, petty, implacable and rightly feared by many. She died in 548. Surviving representations of her show a face with lean cheeks, a high forehead and a haughty stare.

Totila: Benedict's meeting with him. There is no good reason to doubt that such a meeting took place, though Gregory's account (*Dialogue* 14.1–15.2) may be exaggerated in certain ways. Gregory's aim was to show Benedict's powers of clairvoyance, so he says that Totila's lieutenants arrived first, with Totila himself hanging back to see if Benedict would recognise him—which, of course, he did. In fact, it is much more likely that the monks who were watching from the monastery windows—and who were presumably the source of the story—could not tell one gaudy battledress from another and it was they who confused the identity of the visitors. It is also possible that the lieutenants had come on ahead to see if they could do a little opportunistic thieving before their leader arrived and that Totila rode hard to catch them up precisely to stop this happening. Benedict showed some bravery in waiting at the gate to meet the Goths. He had no idea how the encounter would turn out and he seems to have decided that if any life had to be sacrificed to save the community, it would be his.

Why did Totila request a meeting with Benedict? He could not have read the *Rule* and he must, therefore, have been attracted by what he had heard of Benedict's personality. Several of Benedict's personal qualities were on display at this meeting: his calmness, his reasonable approach to problems (it seems that the two of them sat and talked for some considerable time), his tenderness (shown in the way he stepped forward to help Totila rise from his prostration), and his firm principles (he clearly did not pull any punches when the conversation moved on to the subject of the war). Characteristically, the meeting ended in prayer.

Saint Benedict in his Community

One has to read a little between the lines of the account, for Gregory was biased against the Goths; he grew up in a Rome that had been ravaged by war and he blamed the Goths for it. The three Goths that appear in the second *Dialogue* display different negative emotions—timidity, anger and malevolence—and they therefore perpetuate the Roman belief that barbarians were ruled by the passions, unlike Romans, whose lives were governed by rationality. Totila also appears in *Dialogue 3* (at 6, 11 and 12) where he is again portrayed unfavourably.

A. Mundó, 'Sur la date de la visite de Totila à Saint Benoit' in *Revue bénédictine* 59 (1949), pp. 203–6 believes that the visit to Benedict took place in 546. His argument is based on an excessively literal reading of the words attributed to Benedict by Gregory and his conclusion is therefore unconvincing. In fact, it is unlikely that Totila moved away from Rome in 546 because he was preoccupied with the siege of the city, which required his close personal supervision. He made a short visit to the south early in 547, but he was in a hurry to retrieve the military situation in Lucania and Bruttium and he wouldn't have wanted to waste time en route. His earlier expedition to Naples is therefore much the most likely occasion for the meeting with Benedict and the date must be either late in 542 or early in 543.

Totila's personality. Thanks to Gregory, it is easy to imagine Totila as some sort of Hollywood barbarian, with lusty appetites and an evil leer. There are indeed some episodes in Procopius's history of the war that cast Totila in an unfavourable light. For example, Procopius said that the sack of Tivoli and the slaughter of its inhabitants was too dreadful for him to describe, though it is not clear whether Totila was actually present or whether, in the absence of clear orders, his army ran amock, as the armies of those days often did in captured towns. In spite of this, Totila is one of the very few people to emerge with any credit from Procopius's history, even though he and Procopius were on opposite sides in the conflict. In addition to his tactical flair, Totila had a realistic strategy: he knew that

Visitors to the monastery

the Goths could not beat off the imperial armies indefinitely and that a negotiated peace was the best hope of keeping some degree of political independence. He made repeated overtures to Justianian, but these were always rebuffed; Justinian was determined to fight the war to a finish.

On the whole Totila had a reputation for being humane in his dealings with prisoners and non-combatants. Many of his prisoners switched sides and fought in the Gothic ranks. When Totila occupied Rome he ordered his troops to be respectful to women and he won praise for his moderate treatment of the city's elite. When he captured Naples in 543 he realised that the starving inhabitants would probably kill themselves if they ate too much of the food that had suddenly become available, so he instituted a system of rationing, starting with small portions that gradually increased day by day.

Totila also seems to have had firm religious and moral principles. When he entered Rome in 546, his first act was to go and pray in St Peter's. He adhered to the Gothic policy of religious toleration. He insisted that fighting a war did not mean the suspension of moral values. On one occasion he had to rule on the case of a Gothic guard who had raped a local girl. The man was popular with the troops and a delegation came to Totila to ask that he be spared any punishment. Totila replied that victory for the Goths would be no victory if it involved the suspension of moral standards and the endorsement of the sinful acts of individual soldiers; God would not bless their endeavours. The man was executed and his money was handed to the girl. When Totila asked to meet Benedict it is entirely possible that, rather than having the silly motives attributed to him by Gregory, Totila was genuinely attracted by Benedict's holiness and wanted to have a serious discussion about spiritual matters.

Visitors to the monastery. Benedict says (*RB* 53.2) that proper honour should be shown to all visitors, especially *domestici fidei et peregrini*. Various translations of these words are possible. The problem is to emphasise some visitors without ruling out others, which would run the risk of ignoring Christ's own precept—'I was a stranger and you welcomed me' (Mt 25:35)—and Benedict's injunction that honour must be shown 'to all'. *Domestici fidei* could be translated as 'members of the household of faith'. In Rome or a provincial town that would have meant the 'household' of a particular church, those people who were part of its regular congregation, involved in its social networks and entitled to its charitable support. In the context of Monte Cassino this might mean *a.* visiting monks from Benedict's other monastic foundations at Subiaco and Terracina; *b.* important lay families who had supported the monastery through donations and oblations; and *c.* local people who contributed to the daily life of the community and worshipped occasionally with the monks at the mountain-top shrine of St John—people ranging from the Bishop of Aquinum to the mulateers who brought supplies up to the monastery from the plain.

One of the meanings of *peregrini* was 'strangers'. In Rome, this was an administrative category of people who were expelled from the city in times of famine because they were not registered as citizens and therefore not entitled to charitable assistance. By joining such a rejected class of people with those who were closest to the community, Benedict has covered the widest possible range of visitors to the monastery and been faithful to the precept of Christ. The word *peregrini* can also be translated as 'pilgrims', or as 'foreigners' or as 'people far from home' and in *RB* 53.15 it is associated with 'the poor', all of which is consistent with the idea that the monastery was giving shelter to refugees, as well as to pilgrims, visiting monks and pious Christians.

Some commentaries on this chapter argue that *domestici fidei* refers to the whole membership of the Church and must therefore exclude Arians and pagans. This raises a number of problems, not least its contradiction with Benedict's insistence that honour must be shown 'to all'. A large proportion of the population, especially in the countryside, practised a hybrid

Water supply for monasteries

religion in which a core of paganism was overlaid with a veneer of Christianity; how were the monks to decide whether or not to admit such people? The Arians were, at least, Christian and they would have had little difficulty in joining the community in worship (see my discussion of Arian-Catholic relations in Chapter 3). Benedict himself was willing to give Arians a welcome, as he showed when he received Totila and when he took Zalla, the cruel Gothic landlord, into the monastery and gave him food (*Dialogue* 31.3).

It may be that visitors to the monastery quickly defined themselves. After they had been received, guests were led to prayer and were then expected to sit with one of the superiors and listen to a reading from scripture (*RB* 53.8–9). What Benedict was seeking was a sign that visitors were willing to adapt themselves, if only minimally, to the community's aims and routine; without that, their presence in the monastery would have been seriously disruptive. Some visitors would have fitted in easily; others would have felt uncomfortable in a monastery, would have made this obvious and then either left of their own accord or been politely asked to go. By expecting visitors to adapt their behaviour in return for hospitality, Benedict was discouraging bogus monks in search of a free lunch and encouraging wartime refugees to move on once the immediate danger had passed.

For other discussions of this matter see *RB 1980*, pp. 256–7; Kardong, *Benedict's Rule*, p. 422; A. de Vogüé, 'The meaning of Benedictine hospitality' in *Cistercian Studies* 21 (1986), pp. 186–94: A. Böckmann, *Perspectives on the Rule of St Benedict: Expanding our Hearts in Christ* (Collegeville: Liturgical Press, 2005), pp. 163–213.

Water supply for monasteries. The story of the monks' complaint about the water supply (*Dialogue* 5.1–3) is obviously coloured by the biblical parallel of Num 20:2–13 and Ex 17:1–6, where the Israelites are in the wilderness of Sinai and Moses creates for them the waters of Meribah. The Subiaco story is

Saint Benedict in his Community

also an example of the relationship that ought to exist between an abbot and his monks. Benedict wrote (*RB* 68.2) that if a monk found a task too difficult for him, he should choose an appropriate moment and explain patiently to his superior why he couldn't perform it, which is what the deputation of monks did on this occasion. The abbot, for his part, was to listen to the advice of the brothers, asking even the younger members of the community for an opinion (as Benedict evidently did with Placid), and then reach a decision (*RB* 3.2–3).

In locating the spring, Benedict employed one of the techniques commonly used in Roman times. After choosing a likely place, an unbaked earthenware pot was buried and left overnight; if, by the morning, the pot had begun to disintegrate, water was present. T. Hodge, *Roman Aqueducts and Water Supply* (London: Duckworth, 1993) contains a chapter on digging wells and constructing cisterns. The provision of small-scale water systems for farms and villas is discussed in much fascinating detail in R. Thomas and J. I. Wilson, 'Water supply for Roman farms in Latium and south Etruria' in *Papers of the British School at Rome* 62 (1994), pp. 139–96.

Weather: the extraordinary weather of 536. The quotations come from Cassiodorus, *Variae*, XII, 25, 3 (letter to his deputy, around autumn 537). His description is supported by Procopius (*Wars*, 4.14.5–6) and by contemporaries in Constantinople and Antioch. Similar evidence comes from China. A review of the ancient literary evidence is given by A. Arjava, 'The mystery cloud of 536 CE in the Mediterranean sources' in *Dumbarton Oaks Papers* 59 (2005), pp. 73–94, though Arjava probably makes too much of a Byzantine source that says the clouds were damp; the evidence from Italy says the atmosphere was dry. See also J. D. Gunn, *The Years without Summer: Tracing AD 536 and its Aftermath*, British Archaeological Survey International Series 872 (Oxford: Archaeopress, 2000). Modern dendochronology and ice-core data show that there was an abrupt reduction in temperature in 536, followed by a brief recovery and then an even steeper fall in 540, with a slow recovery to 545. Tree-ring growth was 25% below normal in 540 and it has been estimated that the sun was ten times fainter. An obvious explanation for this would be a high cloud of dust, shutting out light and warmth; Cassiodorus describes the sky as filled 'by some sort of mixture ... as if with a kind of tautened skin' (*Variae*, XII. 25, 6). There is now general agreement that volcanoes were responsible for the dust-cloud: a massive northerly eruption in 536, perhaps in Alaska or Iceland, followed by equally large one in 540–1 at a tropical latitude. These eruptions must have been enormous; the largest in recent times, that of Tambora in 1815, produced a year without a summer in 1816 but did not reproduce the stunted tree-ring pattern of 536–45. The identity of the volcanoes has been debated, so far inconclusively, in articles on-line. See also Harper, *Fate of Rome*, pp. 249–59.

In the case of Italy, a link between the dust cloud and crop failure is not easy to show, because the latter has to be distinguished from the effects of war. There was certainly a famine in North Italy and Campania in 537 and in the case of the latter, at least, the situation was exacerbated by military activity. There was a dreadful famine in Tuscany, Umbria and the Marche in 539; Procopius gives a graphic description (*Wars*, 6.20.15–33), but attributes it to disease and the displacement of the population by war. D. Stathakopoulos, *Famine and Pestilence in the Late Roman and Early Byzantine Empire* (Burlington, VT: Ashgate, 2004), pp. 261–300 provides a list of all known famines in the sixth century.

Writing tablets. Some sixth-century examples discovered by archaeologists in Ireland were made of wood about 7 mm thick (about the thickness of a modern pencil) with a surface area of 210 mm x 75 mm (which, by a curious coincidence, is exactly the size of a modern sheet of A5 paper folded lengthways). One side was covered with wax so that it could be written on, except that a small bump of wood was left in the centre so that when the tablets were folded together the wax did not smear.

Saint Benedict in his Community

The wax could, of course, be wiped clean after the words had been memorised or copied on to parchment. The tablets were joined together with leather thongs at the top corners to form bunches, usually of about six, which could be stood on their ends in a semi-circle to form a polyptych.

NOTES

For more extensive information on topics highlighted in bold, please refer to the preceding section: Excursuses.

1. Saint Benedict in his Times

[1] The life of Benedict is the second of four dialogues; for a translation of all four see Gregory the Great, *Dialogues*, trans. O. J. Zimmerman (Washington: Catholic University of America Press, 1959). Translations of the second dialogue have been published separately. Two which have commentaries are T. G. Kardong, *The Life of Saint Benedict by Gregory the Great: Translation and Commentary* (Collegeville: Liturgical Press, 2009) and *The Life of St Benedict*, trans. H. Costello and E. de Bhaldraithe, with a commentary by A. de Vogüé (Petersham, MA: St Bede's Publications, 1993), hereafter cited as de Vogüé, *Life*. My quotations are from Kardong's translation. The years 480 and 547 are generally accepted as approximate dates for the birth and death of Benedict and though they are only educated guesses, I see no good reason to dispute them. The historicity of Benedict is discussed by de Vogüé, *A Critical Study of the Rule of Benedict*, 2 vols (New York: New City Press, 2013), I, pp. 94–105. See **Gregory the Great**.

[2] For example, P. A. Cusack, *An Interpretation of the Second Dialogue of Gregory the Great: Hagiography and St Benedict* (Lewiston/Lampeter: Edwin Mellen Press, 1993). See **Gregory, Dialogues: authenticity**.

[3] Benedict's *Rule*: translations and commentaries have multiplied in recent years. An authoritative translation by a committee of North American scholars is T. M. Fry, ed., *RB 1980; The Rule of St Benedict in Latin and English with Notes* (Collegeville: Liturgical Press, 1981), which also contains lengthy background essays, a detailed index and a concordance of Latin words (this is hereafter referred to as *RB 1980*) Other versions which provide both Latin and English texts, with notes on the translation and a commentary on the *Rule* are Georg Holzherr, *The Rule of Benedict: A Guide to Christian Living; the Full Text of the Rule in Latin and English*, with commentary by Holzherr, translated by the monks of Glenstal Abbey (Blackrock: Four Courts Press, 1994) and Terrence G. Kardong, *Benedict's Rule: A Translation and Commentary* (Collegeville; Liturgical Press, 1996); the latter is very detailed and contains a lengthy bibliography. Abbot Parry, *The Rule of Saint Benedict* (Leominster: Gracewing, 1990) is a translation with an introduction and commentary by Esther de Waal. My quotations are taken from Parry's translation; I am grateful to the copyright holders for allowing me to do this. A translation by a non-monastic author

209

Saint Benedict in his Community

is Carolinne White, *The Rule of Benedict* (London: Penguin Books, 2008). E. de Waal, *Seeking God* (London: Fount/HarperCollins, 1984 and many reprints) has been widely praised as an introduction to Benedictine spirituality; among the other notable modern writers on the subject are Aquinata Böckmann, Michael Casey, Columba Stewart and Adalbert de Vogüé. Joan Chittister, *The Rule of Benedict: Insights for the Ages* (New York: Crossroads, 1992 and many reprints) divides the *Rule* into the portions read day by day in Benedictine communities and gives a challenging and contemporary commentary on each.

2. Roman Italy under Gothic Rule

1 See **The Roman emperors of those times**.
2 See **Theoderic**.
3 For a detailed discussion of this issue see T.S. Burns, 'Calculating Ostrogothic population' in *Acta Antiqua Academiae Scientiarum Hungaricae* 26 (1978), pp. 457–63. The history of Ostrogothic Italy is well described in J. J. O'Donnell, *The Ruin of the Roman Empire* (London: Profile Books, 2009). See also J. J. Arnold, M. S. Bjornlie and K. Sessa, eds, *A Companion to Ostrogothic Italy* (Leiden: Brill, 2016); P. Amory, *People and Society in Ostrogothic Italy, 489–554* (Cambridge: Cambridge University Press, 1997) and the contribution of various authors to A. Cameron, B. Ward-Perkins and M. Whitby, eds, *The Cambridge Ancient History*, vol. XIV (Cambridge: Cambridge University Press, 2000).
4 Benedict's social status is indicated by his education in Rome. It was normal for the provincial elites to send their sons for higher education in the city; as this was expensive, Benedict's father must have been relatively well-to-do. This social class, known as *curiales*, was responsible for collecting and underwriting the government's taxes and levies — an ominous responsibility, because in years of poverty, when the peasants couldn't pay their dues, the curials had to stump up the money themselves. Fortunately this doesn't seem to have happened often and arrears, if they occurred, might eventually be written off. Curials increasingly disliked the pettifogging aspects of civic life and hoped that by seeking higher office and raising their social status they might escape their curial obligations entirely.
5 D. Knowles, *Saints and Scholars* (Cambridge: Cambridge University Press, 1962), p. 6.
6 See **The Gothic kings of those times**.
7 See **Justinian; Theodora**.
8 See **Belisarius**.
9 There is a good brief account of the war in P. J. Heather, *The Restoration of Rome: Barbarian Popes and Imperial Pretenders* (London: Pan Books, 2014), ch. 4. All histories of the war depend heavily on the contemporary account written by Procopius. This has been translated by H. B. Dewing in the Loeb Classical Series and revised by A.

Notes, ch. 3. Religious Life under Gothic Rule

Kaldellis as *The Wars of Justinian / Prokopios* (Indianapolis: Hackett Publishing, 2014). See **Procopius**.

10   See **Totila: Benedict's meeting with him**; **Totila's personality**.
11   See **Rome: a plan for its destruction**.
12   See **East and West**.
13   See **Cassiodorus**.
14   The quotation is from P. Heather, *The Goths* (Oxford: Blackwell, 1996), p. 272. Somewhat different conclusions have been drawn by J. Moorhead, 'Italian loyalties during Justinian's Gothic war' in *Byzantion* 53 (1983), pp. 575–96 and E. A. Thompson, *Romans and Barbarians: The Decline of the Western Empire* (Madison: University of Wisconsin Press, 1982), ch. 6. I am inclined to think that Heather is best supported by the evidence, which in all three cases comes mainly from Procopius.
15   Cassiodorus to Valerianus, *c.* July 536, *Variae*, xii.5.3, trans. S. J. B. Barnish (Liverpool: Liverpool University Press, 1992).
16   See **Visitors to the monastery**.
17   The first quotation is from Cassiodorus to Ambrosius, around autumn 537, *Variae*, xii.25.6; the second is from Procopius, *Wars*, 4.14.5. The dust veil of 536 is discussed in **Weather: the extraordinary weather of 536**. The largest comets were seen in 518, 530 and 539 and their precise dating makes it unlikely that they were three reports of the same event. The comet of 530 was described as 'a tremendous star in the western region, sending a white beam upwards; its surface emitted flashes of lightning … it continued shining for 20 days and there were droughts and murders during riots in every city and many other events full of ill omen' (John Malalas, *The Chronicle of John Malalas*, trans. E. Jeffreys *et al.* (Melbourne: Australian Association of Byzantine Studies, 1986), xviii, p. 52). Vesuvius had erupted three times in living memory, the eruption of 476 producing a volcanic cloud so large that it dropped ash on the roofs of Constantinople.
18   See **Plague: diagnosing the plague**.

3. Religious Life under Gothic Rule

1   This has been stated explicitly by A. Böckmann, who says: 'The Gothic wars were also religious wars'; *Perspectives on the Rule of St Benedict: Expanding our Hearts in Christ* (Collegeville: Liturgical Press, 2005), p. 2. De Vogüé goes further, saying 'This religious barrier, which separated [Totila and the Goths] from the Catholic Romans, was the root cause of the Italian drama' and he sees the Catholic Romans as having been 'oppressed, humiliated and crushed for half a century by occupation and war'; *Life*, p. 83.
2   The mosaics survived until 1598, when the apse of the church collapsed, bringing the mosaics down with it, but detailed drawings had been made earlier and these have survived in church records.

Saint Benedict in his Community

They are discussed in R. W. Mathisen, 'Ricimer's church in Rome: how an Arian barbarian prospered in a Nicene world' in A. Cain and N. Lenski, eds, *The Power of Religion in Late Antiquity* (Farnham: Ashgate, 2009), pp. 307–25. Mathisen sees no distinctively Arian theology in the mosaics.

3 See **Sant' Apollinare Nuovo mosaics**.
4 Quoted by A. Urbano, 'Donation, dedication and *damnatio memoriae*: the Catholic reconciliation of Ravenna and the Church of Sant' Apollinare Nuovo', in *Journal of Early Christian Studies* 13 (2005), p. 97, fn. 71.
5 K. Schaferdiek, 'Germanic and Celtic Christianities' in A. Casiday and F. W. Norris, eds, *The Cambridge History of Christianity: vol. 2, Constantine to c. 600* (Cambridge: Cambridge University Press, 2007), p. 57. See also the various articles in G. M. Berndt and R. Steinacher, eds, *Arianism: Roman Heresy and Barbarian Creed* (Farnham: Ashgate, 2014).
6 Theodoret, *Historia Ecclesiastica*, IV, 37 quoted in J. Stevenson, ed., *Creeds, Councils ad Controversies: Documents Illustrating the History of the Church, A.D. 337–461* (London: SPCK, 1989), p. 38. The quotation in the next sentence is from the Arian bishop Maximinus in the debate between himself and Augustine, trans. R. J. Teske in J. E. Rotelle, ed., *Arianism and other heresies* (Hyde Park, NY: New York City Press, 1995), pp. 205–6. Information about Arianism can also be found in D. Rankin, 'Arianism' in P. F. Esler, ed., *The Early Christian World* (London: Routledge, 2000), vol. 2, pp. 975–1001; R. P. C. Hanson, *The Search for the Christian Doctrine of God: The Arian Controversy 318–381* (Edinburgh: T. T. Clark, 1988); and M. Wiles, *Archetypal Heresy: Arianism through the Centuries* (Oxford: Clarendon Press, 1996).
7 This suggestion is made by M.-G. Dubois, 'The place of Christ in Benedictine spirituality' in *Cistercian Studies* 24 (1989), p. 109, and A. Borias, 'Christ and the monk' in *Monastic Studies* 10 (1974), p. 116. It is Borias who uses the phrase 'militant anti-Arianism', though he gives no justification for the use of the word 'militant'. The places in the *Rule* where the name 'Jesus' is deliberately omitted are 2.20 (from Gal 3:28) and 25.4 (from 1 Cor 5:5).
8 Quoted by D. M. Deliyannis, *Ravenna in Late Antiquity* (Cambridge: Cambridge University Press, 2010), p. 142. The contemporary comments in the previous sentences are quoted by J. Moorhead, *Theoderic in Italy* (Oxford: Clarendon Press, 1992), p. 93.
9 See **Manichaeism**.
10 See **The Ostrogothic succession crisis; Boethius**.
11 See **The popes of those times**.
12 Justinian's threatening message to Amalasuntha is reported by Procopius in *Wars*, 5.3.17–18; his deal with Theodahad (on which the latter reneged) is at *Wars*, 5.6.2–11; and Belisarius's statement to the Neapolitans is at *Wars*, 5.8.13.
13 Procopius, *Wars*, 6.4.9–10.
14 Procopius, *Wars*, 6.6.4–34. This passage reads like an eye-witness account, which it probably was, since Procopius, as Belisarius's legal adviser, would almost certainly have been present. The leader of the

Notes, ch. 4. Benedict as a Student

ambassadors was 'a Roman of note among the Goths', obviously one of those senators (and Catholics) who were still in service at the court in Ravenna. The ambassadors' words were: 'We have so scrupulously guarded for the Romans their practices pertaining to the worship of God and faith in him, that to this day not one of the Italians has changed his belief, either willingly or unwillingly, and when Goths have changed it, we paid no attention. The sanctuaries of the Romans have received from us the highest honour. No one who has taken refuge in any of them has ever been treated with violence by anyone' (18–19).

4. Benedict as a Student

[1] Cassiodorus, *Variae*, 10.30 and 4.51. R. Krautheimer, *Rome: Profile of a City, 312–1308* (Princeton University Press, 1980) is a useful introduction to the city's history.

[2] H. Marrou, *A History of Education in Antiquity*, trans. G. Lamb (New York: Sheed and Ward, 1956), p. 288.

[3] S. Gersh, *Middle Platonism and Neoplatonism: the Latin Tradition*, vol. 2 (Notre Dame: University of Notre Dame Press, 1986), pp. 602, 616.

[4] Virgil, *The Pastoral Poems*, trans. E. V. Rieu (Harmondsworth: Penguin Books, 1954), IV, 7.

[5] See **Benedict's vision**.

[6] See **Proba**.

[7] See **Hymns from the fifth century**.

[8] The quotation comes from Cassiodorus, *An Introduction to Divine and Human Readings*, trans. L. W. Jones (New York: Columbia University Press, 1946), p. 122. Cassiodorus knew Dionysius personally and was also in a good position to assess his wider influence. Unfortunately there are now only scraps of information about 'Denis the Little'. See **Dionysius Exiguus**.

[9] *City of God*, 8.10, trans. H. Bettenson (London: Penguin, 2003), p. 311.

[10] See **Augustine**.

[11] There were three florilegia of Augustine in circulation: relatively short ones by Prosper of Aquitaine and Vincent of Lerins and a much longer one by Eugippius of Lucullanum. Prosper's work contained about 390 passages, mostly about 3–5 lines long. Eugippius's had about 350 extracts, some running to 10 pages, with the whole collection amounting to 1100 pages. Some of the extracts gathered together Augustine's comments on particular books of scripture, but most were organised thematically, with answers to theological questions on issues such as salvation, the trinity and so on. The works from which the extracts were taken are listed by A. Furst in K. Pollmann, ed., *The Oxford Guide to the Reception of Augustine* (Oxford: Oxford University Press, 2013), vol. 2, pp. 955–97. The passages in the *Rule* that most show the influence of Augustine are listed in *RB 1980*,

pp. 594–5. The differences between the two lists are so great that, even after making reasonable allowance for omissions and mistakes, it seems very likely that Benedict did not rely on the florilegia alone but read some of Augustine's works in the original.

12   See **Writing tablets**.

13   The Latin text is *certis iterum horis in lectione divina*. Some translators leave the last two words in Latin, but this seems to me to run the risk of identifying Benedict's instructions with the modern practice of *lectio divina*, which is often a group activity with well-defined structures and outcomes. The modern practice has many benefits but it is not what went on in Benedict's monastery. A literal translation would be 'divine reading' referring 'in the first instance to the nature or quality of the text being read' and secondly to the meditative and reflective approach used by the reader (*RB 1980*, p. 248). 'Prayerful reading' is the translation preferred by *RB 1980*.

14   See **Libraries/*Bibliotheca***.

15   See **Libraries**.

16   See **The codex**.

17   M. Vessey, introduction to Cassiodorus, *Institutions of Divine and Secular Learning*, trans. J. W. Halporn (Liverpool: Liverpool University Press, 2004), pp. 49–51. Cassiodorus wrote (*Institutions*, 1.11.3) that he had gathered 'the Holy Scripture into nine *codices* together with the introductory writers and ... almost all Latin commentators'. It would clearly have been impossible to compress all this material into just nine volumes, so it is likely that only a part of it was bound with the biblical text and the rest was bound separately but cross-referenced to, and shelved with, the appropriate biblical volumes.

18   P. T. R. Gray, '"The Select Fathers": canonising the patristic past' in *Studia Patristica* 23 (1989), pp. 21–36.

19   The quotation from Cassiodorus comes from *Institutions*, 2.27.1. The suggestion that Benedict 'confined' his monks to a narrow syllabus of scripture and commentaries is made by J. G. Clark, *The Benedictines in the Middle Ages* (Woodbridge: Boydell, 2011), p. 195, though Clark goes on to say (p. 196) that this 'must surely have inclined them to intellectual enquiry'. Kardong, *Benedict's Rule*, p. 400, believes that, for Benedict, '*lectio* was almost exclusively tied to the Bible itself'. Abbot Rancé, the great Cistercian reformer of the 17th century, was similarly inclined towards a minimalist diet of Scripture, but in practice, when it came to listing the titles that his monks ought to have at hand, his library expanded rapidly; see D. N. Bell, 'Armand-Jean de Rancé on reading: what, why and how?' in *Cistercian Studies Quarterly* 50 (2015), pp. 161–93.

5. Benedict Leaves Rome

1. 'Fine men' is the translation preferred by Kardong, *Life*, p.2. It incorporates the ideas of 'devout', 'high-standing' and 'nobility' which are favoured by other translators.
2. Unfortunately the Gelineau/Grail translation of the Psalms is very free at this point; it does not use the word 'vessel' and instead refers to 'a thing thrown away'. The Latin *vas* (vessel) is the word used by Gregory in the *Dialogue* and by the Vulgate translation of the Psalms, a version in general use at that time, so the similarity between the two would have been obvious to Gregory's readers. 'Vessel' is the word used in most translations of the Bible and in Anglican psalters. For 'sieve' Gregory uses the Latin *capisterium*, a highly unusual word and a borrowing from the vocabulary of agriculture, meaning 'a winnowing fan'. It is possible that Gregory wished to emphasise the idea of good grain being separated from chaff and therefore, by analogy, of Benedict being winnowed from his fellow students or of Benedict as a future winnower of monks from men.

6. The Church Divided

1. There are many books on the Christological dispute. A very useful reference work is J. A. McGuckin, *The SCM Press A-Z of Patristic Theology* (London: SCM Press, 2005). The theological issues are well described by D. N. Bell, *A Cloud of Witnesses: An Introduction to the Development of Christian Doctrine to AD 500* (Kalamazoo: Cistercian Studies, 2007), which is concise and very engagingly written, and J. A. McGuckin, *The Path of Christianity: The First Thousand Years* (Downers Grove, IL: IVP Press, 2017), pp. 539–603, which includes translations of some of the major documents. A. Grillmeier, *Christ in Christian Tradition*, 2 vols (London: Mowbray, 1975) discusses the subject in great detail. H. Chadwick, *The Early Church* (London: Penguin Books, 1993) puts the theological issues into their historical setting, as does W. H. C. Frend, *The Rise of Christianity* (London: Darton, Longman and Todd, 1984).
2. Cyril to Nestorius, November 430, *Ep.* 17, 8, known as the Third Letter to Nestorius, translated in J. A. McGuckin, *Saint Cyril of Alexandria: The Christological Controversy — Its History, Theology and Texts* (Leiden: Brill, 1994), pp. 266–75.
3. Cyril to Nestorius, November 430, *Ep.* 17, 3, McGuckin, p. 268. See **Cyril of Alexandria**.
4. Cyril to John of Antioch, Spring 433, *Ep.*39, 8, translated in McGuckin, *Saint Cyril*, pp. 343–8. The word 'nature' is now generally used in translating this formula, but Cyril himself often used 'hypostasis' (individual reality). The controversy between East and West was

Saint Benedict in his Community

sharpened by the difficulty of translating terms such as 'nature', 'person' and 'hypostasis' between Greek and Latin.

[5] A translation of the *Dogmatic Definition of the Council of Chalcedon* is in McGuckin, *Path of Christianity*, pp. 593–5.

[6] A. Grillmeier, *Christ in Christian Tradition*, vol. 2, *From the Council of Chalcedon (451) to Gregory the Great (590–604)*, pt 1, trans. P. Allen and J. Cawte (London: Mowbray, 1987), p. 255.

[7] *Ibid.*, p. 295.

[8] The schism has been discussed by many historians. See particularly K. Sessa, *The Formation of Papal Authority in Late Antique Italy: Roman Bishops and the Domestic Sphere* (New York: Cambridge University Press, 2013); J. Richards, *The Popes and the Papacy in the Early Middle Ages, 476–752* (London: Routledge and Kegan Paul, 1979); Moorhead, *Theoderic in Italy*; P. Llewellyn, 'The Roman clergy during the Laurentian Schism: a preliminary analysis' in *Ancient Society* 8 (1979), pp. 245–75 and 'The Roman Church during the Laurentian Schism: priests and senators' in *Church History* 45 (1976), pp. 417–27.

[9] Laurentius died soon afterwards in straitened circumstances. He has gone down in history as an 'anti-pope', with all the obloquy that that entails, but he appears to have been a worthy candidate for the papacy and to have behaved with some dignity during the schism. Theoderic's actions may seem to have breached his own rule of non-interference in Church affairs, but, in fact, he tried wherever possible to leave responsibility with the bishops. When, in 506, he finally called a halt to the schism, he was prompted by fear that ecclesiastical disputes would combine with popular discontent arising from a poor harvest. The last thing Theoderic wanted was to have to restore order in Rome himself, using Gothic troops against one of the senatorial factions, which would have been a political disaster.

[10] Modern authors are agreed that Benedict was probably in Rome at the time of the schism, but most of them shy away from considering Benedict's reaction to it. McCann says primly: 'The experience would not edify him. No doubt he knew where truth and right lay and did not hesitate in his allegiance'; J. McCann, *Saint Benedict* (New York: Sheed and Ward, 1937), p. 56. Schuster imagines Benedict in the crowd that greeted Theoderic outside St Peter's during the state visit of 500, but avoids discussing the schism; I. Schuster, *St Benedict and his Times* (St Louis: Herder, 1951), p. 22. De Wohl, in his novel *Citadel of God* (London: Gollacz, 1960), pp. 79–88, pictures Benedict in a procession escorting Symmachus to a synod when it is attacked by the Laurentians: Benedict then decides to withdraw from Rome because the city's factionalism 'opposes tranquillity of mind' (p. 88). This explanation of Benedict's withdrawal is plausible, but I think it is unlikely that Benedict was in the Symmachan camp.

[11] These 'thorns of contention' were rather more than the frictions that naturally occur in communal life. The Latin word is *scandalum, -orum*, which means 'an obstacle which trips one up'. It is generally used in a figurative sense. The translation is from *RB 1980*, which has a useful footnote on the subject, pp. 208–9. See also the entry by G. Stählin in

Notes, ch. 6. The Church Divided

G. Friedrich and G. W. Bromiley, eds, *Theological Dictionary of the New Testament* (Grand Rapids: Eerdmans, 1971), VII, pp. 339–58. Stählin says that in the Bible *scandalum* is used when describing a clash of ideas that leads to a collapse of faith (e.g. in Rom 16:17).

[12] *Dogmatic Definition*, trans. McGuckin, *Path of Christianity*, p. 594.

[13] See **Cassian**.

[14] This has been translated by E. C. S. Gibson as *The Seven Books on the Incarnation of the Lord, Against Nestorius* in H. Ware and P. Schaff, eds, *A Select Library of Nicene and Post-Nicene Fathers of the Church, Second Series, v.11, Sulpitius Severus, Vincent of Lerins, John Cassian* (Oxford and New York: James Parker/Christian Literature Co., 1894). The request to write the book actually came from Leo—later Pope Leo I—who was then archdeacon to Pope Celestine I. *The Incarnation* is often condemned as second-rate theology (e.g. by Grillmeier and by Stewart) though that does not mean that Benedict did not read it. Two recent reappraisals which take a more favourable view of Cassian's Christology are D. Fairbairn, *Grace and Christology in the Early Church* (Oxford: Oxford University Press, 2003) and A. M. Casiday, *Tradition and Theology in St John Cassian* (Oxford: Oxford University Press, 2007).

[15] *Incarnation*, iv, 6.

[16] Cyril, 'Scholia on the Incarnation', trans. McGuckin, *St Cyril*, pp. 296–7.

[17] Sessa, *Formation*, places great emphasis on the household as a model for ecclesiastical organisation, with the bishop in the role of *paterfamilias*. See **Sexual mores and the papacy**.

[18] K. Bowes, *Private Worship, Public Values, and Religious Change in Late Antiquity* (Cambridge: Cambridge University Press, 2008), p. 76.

[19] P. A. B. Llewellyn, 'The Roman church during the Laurentian schism: priests and senators' in *Church History* 45 (1976), p. 420. Much has been written on the *tituli*; see especially K. Bowes, *Private Worship*, pp. 65–71; A. H. M. Jones, 'Church finance in the fifth and sixth centuries' in *Journal of Theological Studies* 11 (1960), pp. 84–94; J. Hillner, 'Families, patronage and the titular churches of Rome, 300–600' in K. Cooper and J. Hillner, eds, *Religion, Dynasty and Patronage in early Christian Rome, 300–900* (Cambridge: Cambridge University Press, 2007), pp. 225–61; P. Brown, *Through the Eye of a Needle: Wealth, the Fall of Rome, and the Making of Christianity in the West, 350–550 AD* (Woodstock: Princeton University Press, 2012).

[20] A particularly striking example of this comes from the countryside near Tivoli, where a wealthy general—who happened also to be a Goth—built a church on his estate and decorated it with silver plate and expensive textiles. But he added a clause to his deed of gift which stated that if a future bishop attempted to alienate any of these objects or transfer them to another church, the whole gift would be null and void and would revert to the general's family; see Brown, *Eye of a Needle*, pp. 469–70.

[21] This change is well described by Brown, *Eye of a Needle*, who also gives references to other works on the supply of food to Rome. A

Saint Benedict in his Community

clear description of the official system (the *annona*) is given by E. Tengstrom, *Bread for the People: Studies of the Corn Supply of Rome during the Late Empire* (Stockholm: Svenska Institutet i Rom, 1974). There are interesting comments on the respective roles of emperor, nobility and Church in C. R. Whittaker, 'Late Roman trade and traders' in P. Garnsey, K. Hopkins and C. R. Whittaker, eds, *Trade and the Ancient Economy* (London: Chatto and Windus, 1983). The huge grain silos that survive in the crypt of Santa Cecilia in Trastevere are visible evidence of the role of the *tituli* in food supply.

[22] Symmachus built alliances—quite literally—through his embellishments at St Peter's, e.g. in the oratory of St Apollinaris of Ravenna, in the oratory of St Sossius of Campania, in the confession of St Cassian of Imola, and in other parts of the cathedral. This meant that dioceses all over Italy began to see St Peter's, rather than the Lateran cathedral, as the focus of their prayers and pilgrimages. Symmachus also built accommodation for his junior clergy alongside St Peter's, which helped to identify the Vatican, rather than the Lateran, as the centre of papal power.

[23] Bowes, *Private Worship*, p. 80.

[24] W. H. C. Frend, *The Rise of the Monophysite Movement* (Cambridge: Cambridge University Press, 1972) gives a very full account of this whole period. For a more succinct account, see P. T. R. Gray, 'The legacy of Chalcedon: Christological problems and their significance' in M. Maas, ed., *The Cambridge Companion to the Age of Justinian* (Cambridge: Cambridge University Press, 2005). pp. 215–38.

[25] The text of the 'Confession' and some background information are to be found in J. A. McGuckin, 'The "Theopaschite Confession" (text and historical context): a study in the Cyrilline re-interpretation of Chalcedon' in *Journal of Ecclesiastical History* 35 (1984), pp. 239–55; also in R. R. McGregor and D. Fairbairn, *Fulgentius of Ruspe and the Scythian Monks: Correspondence on Christology and Grace* (Washington, DC: Catholic University of America Press, 2013), especially the Introduction by Fairbairn. The quotations in the following sentence are taken from McGuckin, pp. 248–50.

[26] 'Explanation 12' of the twelve *anathemata*, McGuckin, *St Cyril*, p. 292. Cyril's twelfth *anathemata* was quoted by the monks in the 'Confession'. The monks' explanation may have made Cyril's position more credible on the vexed question of a suffering Divinity, but it is still not totally convincing (see **Cyril of Alexandria**).

[27] See **Semi-Pelagianism**.

[28] See the discussion by R. Price in *The Acts of the Council of Constantinople of 553 with Related Texts on the Three Chapters Controversy* (Liverpool: Liverpool University Press, 2012), pp. 59–75.

[29] C. Sotinel, 'The Three Chapters and the transformation of Italy' in C. Chazelle and C. Cubitt, eds, *The Crisis of the Oikoumene: The Three Chapters and the Failed Quest for Unity in the Sixth-Century Mediterranean* (Turnhout: Brepols, 2007), p. 120.

Notes, ch. 7. The Monastery in the World

7. The Monastery in the World

1. Benedict was clearly an attractive candidate for abbot—a man of obvious virtue, able to attract others to the monastic life—and he was also likely to attract donations from wealthy supporters. Vicovaro was a depressing place, a series of caves hacked into the cliff face overlooking a gorge of the River Anio. The monks may have thought that Benedict would be able to raise the funds for more comfortable accommodation in a purpose-built monastery. Even if the story of the attempt to poison him (*Dialogue* 3.3–4) is not literally true, it is easy to imagine the monks' disappointment with him.

2. For example, the early chapters of the *Rule of the Four Fsthers* deal with the reception of visitors, travellers and postulants from differing social backgrounds, matters that Benedict must have found problematic in the early years at Subiaco. The needs of a more settled community are considered in the *Regula Orientalis*, which prescribes the appointment of a cellarer and porter (chs. 25–6) and deals with the correction of faults (ch. 32) in a process very similar to that of *RB* 23. See *Early Monastic Rules: The Rules of the Fathers and the Regula Orientalis*, trans. C. V. Franklin, I. Havener and J. Francis (Collegeville: Cistercian Publications, 1981).

3. See **Benedict and the Master**.

4. The lake no longer exists. In Benedict's time there were three dams across the Anio, creating three lakes, the largest of which was in front of Nero's villa, with an access road on arches across the top of the dam. In addition to providing amusement for the emperor, the lake acted as a settling reservoir for a series of tunnels and aqueducts which took water down to the city of Rome. The dam was probably at least 130 feet high and was the highest in the world until the construction of the dam at Alicante in 1594. The dam at Subiaco survived until 1305. See N. A. F. Smith, 'The Roman dams of Subiaco' in *Technology and Culture* 22 (1970), pp. 58–68. Presumably the access road remained useful to local people long after the villa had fallen into ruin and traffic would have come annoyingly close to any monks who were living there.

5. See **Water supply for monasteries**.

6. It seems that the community did try to clear tiny plots of land on the edge of the lake; in doing so, one of the monks lost a sickle in the water while cutting thornbushes (*Dialogue* 6.1–2). On another occasion, the young monk Placid fell into the lake and was rescued by Maur who appeared to walk on water in order to reach him. The biblical model for this story (Mt 14:29–31) is so obvious that it is easy to overlook the fact that it may have had an element of truth. Anyone who's walked through long grass on the edge of a swollen lake will know how difficult it is to distinguish firm land from deep water; a step in one direction and you topple in (cf. Placid), a step in the other and, though water comes up to your ankles, the ground underneath is firm (cf. Maur).

Saint Benedict in his Community

7   Schuster, *Benedict*, p. 115, has an alternative suggestion: the bread was a *eulogia*, a piece of blessed bread sent as a sign of friendship. Either way, the poison can be seen as a metaphor for the conditions that Florentius was trying to attach to his relationship with the community.

8   If the story is intended to be taken literally and Benedict had been worried about the morals of his monks when he was there to supervise them, how much more worried would he have been about the morals of those he left behind after he had gone to Cassino?

9   Legend has it that the site was a gift from Tertullus, a major landowner, who had visited Subiaco, admired Benedict and offered his son, Placid, as an oblate. The details may be questionable, but some such donation is almost certain. L. Tosti, *Saint Benedict: An Historical Discourse on his Life* (London: Kegan Paul, 1896), p. 70.

10 Commentators have sometimes wondered whether Benedict wrote the *Rule* for general circulation. At *RB* 73.1 he says he hopes it will be observed 'in monasteries' and at *RB* 18.22 he seems to envisage a situation in which someone other than himself is in charge. However, it is not necessary to propose a general circulation for the *Rule*. The reason for Benedict's use of the plural must surely be that he had three communities to care for and the *Rule* was part of his abbatial oversight of them.

11 Augustine, *Praeceptum*, 1.8, which became Eugippius, *Rule*, 1.47.

12 A. K. Gometz, 'Eugippius of Lucullanum: A Biography' (Ph.D. thesis, University of Leeds, 2008), p. 169, concludes that 'the evidence for Eugippius acting as a bridge for the transmission of the *Regula Magistri* to Benedict is too strong to ignore'. The influence of Eugippius is also discussed by C. Leyser, *Authority and Asceticism from Augustine to Gregory the Great* (Oxford: Clarendon Press, 2000), pp. 108–28, and others.

Correspondences between the *Rules* of Benedict and the Master are tabulated in *RB 1980*, appendix 7, pp. 478–93 and discussed exhaustively by de Vogüé in his *Critical Study* and elsewhere. Comparisons between particular chapters and verses within the two texts have become the norm in most commentaries. Such comparisons are a valuable way of bringing Benedict's ideas into sharper focus. Pointing to parallel passages in the Master is not, however, an adequate analysis of the historical and cultural background to Benedict's *Rule*; the two texts are too close to each other in time and place for the one to be a sufficient background to the other. What is needed is a broader survey of the historical context that is common to both.

13 The Liri Valley in the Middle Ages' in G. A. Loud, *Montecassino and Benevento in the Middle Ages: Essay in South Italian Church History* (Aldershot, Variorum, 2000), I, pp. 3–4. Clark, *Benedictines*, p.11 confuses this with the situation in Benedict's time.

14 See **Farm management**.

15 See **Sheep farming**.

16 Here I am contradicting de Vogüé, who believes (*Life*, pp. 108–9) that Benedict made a decision never to leave his monastery. Benedict would have been thought very remiss if had not occasionally visited

Notes, ch. 7. The Monastery in the World

his monastic properties and it seems to me wholly beyond belief that he never paid an abbatical visit to the daughter communities at Subiaco and Terracina. De Vogüé is contradicted by the story of the peasant who carried his dead son up Monte Cassino to be revived by Benedict, only to find that he was out in the fields (*Dialogue* 32.1), and by the story of the visit to Scholastica (*Dialogue* 33.2).

17 See **Weather: the extraordinary weather of 536**.
18 Unfortunately, Benedict's economic intelligence deserts him at this point. By setting prices lower than those of workshops in the town, the monastery would have been undercutting them. Nevertheless, it is clear that Benedict's intention was to share the market with local artisans.
19 See **Perfume making**.
20 See **Monks: the number of monks**.
21 The debate is well summarised by Sessa, *Formation*, pp. 63–86 and set into context by Brown, *Eye of a Needle*, pp. 462–77.
22 See **The so-called 'Benedict Option'**.
23 See **Gregory, *Dialogue*, factual evidence in the *Dialogue***.
24 This is one of the conclusions that Peter Brown has drawn from his important studies of the holy man in late antique society; see Brown, 'The saint as exemplar in late Antiquity' in *Representations* 2 (1983), pp. 10–11.
25 Tree worship was common in Campania. There is an echo of this in the number of churches in the region that are dedicated to St Silvanus/Sylvester. See R Lanciani, *Wanderings in the Roman Campania* (London: Constable, 1909), pp. 60–5.
26 The *Dialogue* places great emphasis on the opposition to Benedict (e.g. at *Dialogue* 8.12). The fact that Gregory chose to express this through metaphor does not mean that it was unreal. The point is important because, during the fifth and sixth centuries, monks were coming to be seen as the holy poor, as outsiders and as Others, 'as the primary intercessors for the sins of all Christians ... whose effectiveness derived from their otherness' (Brown, *Eye of a Needle*, pp. 516–17). If Benedict's community was slow to win acceptance among the people of the locality, it is likely that it was slow to be entrusted with this intercessory responsibility. It is also doubtful if the monks could act as 'powerhouses of prayer' in this way. The community offered no Mass, may not have had priests, and had no space in its liturgy or daily timetable for long intercessory prayers. In this respect, Benedict's community belongs to the ancient traditions of monasticism rather than to the newly emerging charism.
27 Schuster, *Benedict*, pp. 142–3, has seized on this reference to preaching to conclude that Benedict was a priest and had a papal licence for missionary work, which, as a monk, he would not normally have been allowed to do. In fact, it is much more likely that Benedict was leading by example.
28 Those are *Dialogue* 8.1–7 (Florentius) and *Dialogue* 16.1–2 (the priest from Aquinum who disobeyed Benedict's orders after his cure). The

Saint Benedict in his Community

exception is the priest who brought an Easter meal to Benedict during his first year in the cave at Subiaco (*Dialogue* 1.6–7).

29 Carole Straw observes that holy men are usually to be found at the intersection between a horizontal axis across society and a vertical axis to God; *Gregory the Great: Perfection in Imperfection* (Berkeley: University of California Press, 1988), p. 94.

30 I have discussed Benedict's social background in Chapter 2 and note 4. The episode with the lamp undermines the legend that Benedict was related in some way to the Anicii, for that was a family at the very apex of Roman society and the young monk, like everyone else, would have been in awe of such a relationship.

31 Justinian, Annotated Justinian Code: Justinian Novels (www.uwyo.edu/lawlib/blume-justinian), N. 5.2–3 of 17 March 535 and 123.17 of 1 May 546.

32 See **Slavery**.

33 R. Knapp, *Invisible Romans* (London: Profile Books, 2013), p. 7. The summing up in the next sentence is from R. Macmullen, *Roman Social Relations, 50 B.C. to A.D. 284* (New Haven: Yale Univeristy Press, 1974), pp. 102–15.

8. The Community at Home

1 See ***Dominus, paterfamilias* and abbot**.

2 Valerius Maximus, *Memorable Doings and Sayings*, ed. and trans. D. R. Shackleton Bailey (Cambridge, MA: Harvard University Press, 2000), 5.7. This and other literary sources are discussed by R. P. Saller, *Patriarchy, Property and Death in the Roman Family* (Cambridge: Cambridge University Press, 1994), pp. 108–10.

3 Saller, *Patriarchy*, p. 131.

4 One of the manuals was written for the so-called *domina* of Bobbio, possibly in about 395–420; see K. Cooper, *The Fall of the Roman Household* (Cambridge: Cambridgte University Press, 2007), pp. 119–22. Another was written in about 440 for Demetrias, a member of the Anicii family, She had originally decided on a life of virginity but later renounced the veil in order to take up management of some of the family estates; see M. K. C. Krabbe, *Epistula ad Demitriadem de Vera Humilitate: A Critical Text and Translation with Introduction and Commentary* (Washington, DC: Catholic University of America Press, 1965). Many of the specific injunctions in these manuals are paralleled in *RB*. The quotations in my text are from *Epistula*, 3, Krabbe, pp. 148–9.

5 *Ad Gregoriam in palatio*, 18. This text is discussed at length by Cooper, *Roman Household*, and a full translation is provided in an appendix. The homily is thought to have been written during the reign of Theoderic.

6 For example, passages in the *Ad Gregoriam* may be compared with *RB* 64: 'show your slaves your compassion and most often grant

Notes, ch. 8. The Community at Home

forgiveness of their offences' (*AG* 19, cf. 64.10); 'your pattern of fair dealing will be the teacher of everyone, from which fair dealing and mercy demand this, that without violation of kindness, it should put away from itself those whose reform must be despaired of' (*AG* 19, cf. 64.14); so treat your slaves that 'they may wish life to a mother and not death to a taskmistress' (*AG* 18, cf. 64.15); 'examine all that you are about to do or say beforehand by a careful consideration within yourself' (*AG* 18, cf. 64.17); and fulfil the duty of moral and spiritual leadership, as described in the previous paragraph of my text.

7 *RB 1980*, Appendix 4, pp. 415–36, is an essay on Benedict's disciplinary measures which concentrates on identifying scriptural sources for all of Benedict's provisions. Benedict knew the Bible so well that these sources probably sprang quickly to mind when he considered the whole question of communal discipline. However, an explanation along these lines alone is not sufficient. Kardong's two 'overviews' of discipline, *Benedict's Rule*, pp. 251–7 and pp. 371–7, are more wide-ranging.

In several places (e.g. *RB* 32.5 and 54.5) Benedict prescribes *disciplina regularis*, the discipline of the *Rule*, to deal with offenders. This phrase has puzzled commentators, since one assumes that following the *Rule* is what monks would normally have been doing. It seems to me that Benedict is here referring to the disciplinary process outlined in *RB* 23. Thus, to be subject to *disciplina regularis* means to be subjected to that process. There are several other places where Benedict refers to the punishment (*correptio*) imposed by the *Rule*, which I take to be the disciplinary process of *RB* 23 without the warnings. The warnings of *RB* 23 are superfluous in those cases because warnings have been separately prescribed in the chapters concerned (e.g. *RB* 33.7–8).

8 See Kardong, *Benedict's Rule*, p. 516, for references.
9 This was obviously a problem for monasteries generally, since it is ruled upon in successive law-codes. See D. Walters, 'From Benedict to Gratian: the code in medieval ecclesiastical authors' in I. Wood, ed., *The Theodosian Code* (1993), p. 201 and Justinian, N. 5.5–6.
10 See **Clothing**.
11 See **Purple**.
12 See **Bread preparation**.
13 In imagining this kitchen work, I have been influenced by the *Moretum*, an anonymous poem of the first century CE, which was written in a realistic style as a corrective to the rose-tinted accounts of rural life in most Latin literature. See *The Ploughman's Lunch: Moretum, a Poem ascribed to Virgil*, edited with a translation, introduction and commentary by E. J. Kenney (Bristol: Bristol Classical Press, 1984). The poem, which is, in fact, almost certainly not by Virgil, describes in great detail how a ploughman ground his corn, made unleavened bread, and prepared a herbal relish before going out to work.
14 See the calculations in *RB 1980*, pp. 238–9.
15 This is a moot point, which has been debated inconclusively by

Saint Benedict in his Community

religious communities over the centuries. See **Meat eating**.
[16] See **Diet: a balanced diet**.
[17] Ovid, *The Metamorphoses of Ovid*, trans. M. M. Innes (Penguin Classics, 1955), VIII, p. 213.
[18] Italians have eaten their bread in soup for centuries. In the 1940s a common dish in peasant households in the area around Monte Cassino was *minestrina*, thin slices of bread placed in a bowl and covered with bean soup.
[19] See **Food production and preservation: handbooks**.
[20] William of St Thierry, *Vita Prima*, I, vii, 35 in P. Matarasso, trans. and ed., *The Cistercian World: Monastic Writings of the Twelfth Century* (London: Penguin Books, 1991), p. 31.

9. Ways of Prayer

[1] Domestic religious activity is described in Bowes, *Private* Worship, pp. 53–4, 75–102; Sessa, *Formation*, pp. 56–7; K. Sessa, *Daily Life in Late Antiquity* (New York: Cambridge University Press, 2018), pp. 198–221. See also K. Bowes, 'Personal devotions and private chapels' in V. Burrus, ed., *Late Antique Christianity* (Minneapolis: Fortress Press, 2005), pp. 188–210.
[2] See P. Bradshaw, *Daily Prayer in the Early Church* (London: SPCK, 1981) and C. Stewart, 'Prayer' in S. A. Harvey and D. G. Hunter, eds, *The Oxford Handbook of Early Christian Studies* (Oxford: Oxford University Press, 2008), pp. 744–63. There are many other sources which touch on the same subject.
[3] Kardong, *Benedict's Rule*, p. 214. Kardong gives a useful summary of the extensive literature on Benedict's liturgy, as does *RB 1980*, Appendix 3, pp. 379–414. The authoritative treatment of the subject is R. Taft, *The Liturgy of the Hours in East and West: The Origins of the Divine Office and Its Meaning for Today* (Collegeville: Liturgical Press, 2nd edn., 1993). See also J. F. Baldovin, 'The Empire baptized' in G. Wainwright and K. B. Westerfield Tucker, eds, *The Oxford History of Christian Worship* (Oxford: Oxford University Press, 2006), pp. 76–130.
[4] See *RB* 9.4, 13.11 and 17.8. Benedict refers more generally to 'hymns' at other points in the Offices, but these are not likely to have been Ambrosian and may have been material such as canticles (e.g. the *Nunc dimittis* at Compline, *RB* 17.10).
[5] See P. Bradshaw, 'Mass' in *Encyclopedia of Early Christianity* (New York and London: Garland, 1997), vol. 2, pp. 737–8. The first certain use of *missa* for Mass is in Cassiodorus's *Commentary on the Psalms*, which he wrote in the 540s while in exile in Constantinople.
[6] Missa/dismissal. The places where *missa* most obviously means 'dismissal' are *RB* 17.4, 5, 8 and 10. The other uses of *missa* are at 35.14, 38.2 and 60.4. In 35.14 *missa* also refers to prayers of dismissal, this time at the end of a meal; see Kardong, *Benedict's Rule*, p. 294

Notes, ch. 9. Ways of Prayer

and Böckmann, *Monastic Table*, p. 122. In 60.4 Benedict uses *missa* when discussing the role of a monk/priest who is standing next to the abbot. This would be a logical place to stand if he was assisting with the prayers of dismissal, but it would be inappropriate if he was celebrating Mass.

7   Missa/Mass. Kardong, *Benedict's Rule*, p. 294 says 'Whether Benedict ever mentions Mass is a matter of scholarly dispute', but he nevertheless translates RB 38.2 as 'Mass'. De Vogüé holds contradictory views. In one place he thinks that 'perhaps Mass was celebrated less often [than weekly], even without fixed regularity' ('Problems of the monastic conventual Mass' in *Downside Review*, 87 (1969), p. 328), but he asserts elsewhere that RB 38.2 is 'clearly a matter of Sunday Mass' (*Critical Study*, 1, p. 61). *RB 1980* discusses all the uses of *missa* in the *Rule*, accepts that 'in none of these instances is it clear beyond all doubt that *missa* means "Mass"' (p. 411), but leans towards de Vogüé's first conclusion and then continues to translate 38.2 as 'Mass'. Some recent translations of the *Rule* use both 'Mass' and 'dismissal' without appearing to notice the inconsistency involved.

8   Communion *extra missam* is well described by de Vogüé in his introduction to L. Eberle, trans., *The Rule of the Master* (Kalamazoo: Cistercian Publications, 1977), pp. 31–2, though he does not seem to have noticed any similarity between this and RB 38.2.

9   Much has been written on the history of reservation; see, for example, G. Dix, *A Detection of Aumbries: with Other Notes on the History of Reservation* (London: Dacre Press, 1942).

10 Taft, *Liturgy of the Hours*, p.305 is adamant on this point: 'Before the Western Middle Ages no one would have dreamt of preferring daily private Mass to the common hours on weekdays'.

11 See Gregory's letter to John, Bishop of Ravenna, September 594, *The Letters of Gregory the Great*, trans. J. R. C. Martyn, 3 vols (Toronto: Pontifical Institute of Medieval Studies, 2004), II, 5.1.

12 Kardong, *Benedict's Rule*, pp. 505–6, is one of the very few people to translate the reflexive pronoun *sibi* (for himself) in RB 62.1 Parry has 'for his service'. Most translators get round the problem of the pronoun's interpretation by deleting it. Kardong rightly believes that Benedict intended the monk/priest to prevent 'the domination of the neighboring clergy or bishop'.

13 See P. Brown, *The Body and Society: Men, Women and Sexual Renunciation in Early Christianity* (New York: Columbia University Press, 2008), pp. 259–84: B. P. McGuire, 'The Cistercians and the Transformation of Monastic Friendship' in *Analecta Cisterciensia* 37 (1981), p. 24. For example, there is the relationship between Melania the Elder and the emotionally broken Evagrius when he arrived in Jerusalem from Constantinople. Stewart has summed up the importance of this well: 'Genuine commitment to monastic *conversatio* means the kind of accountability possible only when one human being opens the heart to another and experiences forgiving acceptance'; *Prayer and Community: The Benedictine Tradition* (London: Darton, Longman and Todd, 1998), p. 101.

Saint Benedict in his Community

[14] Gregory the Great's aunts are mentioned in his *Dialogue* 4.16; the abbess of Spoleto is in *Dialogue* 3.21. For information on small communities see J. A. McNamara, 'Muffled voices: the lives of consecrated women in the fourth century' in J. A. Nichols and L. T. Shank, eds, *Medieval Religious Women: Distant Echoes*, I (Kalamazoo: Cistercian Publications, 1984), II-29. The wealthy leaders of female asceticism *c.* 400 CE are described in J. M Petersen, *Handmaids of the Lord: Contemporary Descriptions of Feminine Asceticism in the First Six Christian Centuries* (Kalamazoo: Cistercian Publications, 1996).

[15] When the abbey at Monte Cassino was being restored after its destruction in World War Two, a pair of tombs was discovered under the oratory, which would seem to confirm Benedict's request that he and Scholastica should rest together after their deaths (*Dialogue* 34.2 and 37.4).

[16] P. A. Cusack, 'St Scholastica: myth or real person?' in *Downside Review* 92 (1974), p. 158. Cusak concludes that Scholastica was a real person — rather surprisingly, since most of his article leads to the conclusion that the incidents in the *Dialogue* 'are all themes, not facts' (p. 157).

[17] Even then, Benedict makes it clear in v.47 that the strictness should be balanced and reasonable and directed towards 'wiping out faults and preserving love'; see Böckmann's lengthy comment on the verse in *Perspectives*, pp. 37–8.

[18] For contrasting interpretations of this episode see J. H. Wansbrough, 'St Gregory's intention in the stories of St Scholastica and St Benedict' in *Revue bénédictine* 75 (1965), pp. 145–51, and A. de Vogüé, 'The Meeting of Benedict and Scholastica: An Interpretation' in *Cistercian Studies* 18 (1983), pp. 167–83. Wansbrough thinks this story illustrates contemplation, de Vogüé thinks it is about love. I do not see why it cannot be about both. De Vogüé also thinks it shows the triumph of love over the prescriptions of the *Rule*. It is true that Benedict might have been in breach of several rules — 66.7 on being outside the monastic enclosure, 51.1 on eating outside the monastery and 50.1 on missing the offices — but as abbot he had the authority to relax any of these regulations.

[19] John Cassian, *The Conferences*, trans. B. Ramsey (Mahwah, NJ: Newman Press, 1997), 9.26–30: C. Stewart, *Cassian the Monk* (New York: Oxford University Press, 1998), pp. 123–8. Cassian makes clear that the music of psalmody could be as affecting as the words.

[20] *Dialogue 3*, 34.2 as quoted by B. and P. F. McGinn, *Early Christian Mystics: The Divine Vision of the Spiritual Masters* (New York: Crossroad, 2005), p. 81.

[21] See *RB 1980*, pp. 198, 416–19: A Böckmann, *From the Tools of Good Works to the Heart of Humility: A Commentary on Chapters 4–7 of Benedict's Rule* (Collegeville: Liturgical Press, 2017), pp. 50–5, 184–5; O. D. Watkins, *A History of Penance, v.2, The Western Church from AD 450 to AD 1215* (London: Longmans Green, 1920); M. De Jong, 'Transformations of penance' in P. Theuws and J. L. Nelson, *Rituals of Power, from Late Antiquity to the Early Middle Ages* (Leiden: Brill, 2000), pp. 185–224.

[22] Benedict's uses of 'heart' (*cor*) are listed in *RB 1980*, pp. 506–7. See

Notes, ch. 9. Ways of Prayer

also M. Casey, '*Intentio Cordis* (RB 52:4)' in *Regulae Benedicti Studia* 6/7 (1981), pp. 105–20. *RB 1980* translates this phrase as 'heartfelt devotion'; White, *Rule*, translates it as 'spiritual concentration', Parry, *Rule*, as 'attention' of the heart. These translations capture something of its meaning, but, as Casey points out, the phrase must 'be understood by appreciating all the alternative connotations' (p. 116).

23 Cassian's reference to Mt 5:8 is in *Conference* 1.10.4. His main writings on prayer are in *Conferences* 9 and 10. In 9.18.1 he says that 'a still more sublime and exalted condition follows upon [the four kinds of prayer]. It is fashioned by the contemplation of God alone and by fervent charity, by which the mind, having been dissolved and flung into love of him, speaks most familiarly and with particular devotion to God as to its own father' (Ramsey's translation). There is a longer and very beautiful description of contemplation in 10.6.1–7.2.

24 Krabbe, *Epistula ad Demitriadem*, 4, p. 151. The major book on the subject was *De Vita Contempliva*, by Julianus Pomerius (died *c.* 500). This is discussed by R. A. Markus, *The End of Ancient Christianity* (Cambridge: Cambridge University Press, 1990), pp. 189–92

25 I have chosen the Coverdale/AV translation of the psalm because it seems to me to convey better than many modern translations how Benedict would have understood the psalm. The translation of v.2 is problematic because of changes in the meaning of the word *iustitia*; see *RB 1980*, p. 161, fn. 25.

26 *Dialogue 1*, preface 1, in McGinn's translation, *Early Christian Mystics*, pp. 77–8.

27 Cassian, *Conferences*, 1.15.1–3. The Master's text (*RM* Ths. 19 ff.) is the same as Benedict's. This is one of the parts of his *Rule* which Benedict borrowed almost verbatim—almost, but not completely, for the crucial last verses of Benedict's Prologue (vv.46–9) are Benedict's own words. Benedict follows Cassian in showing that a degree of unity with God can be achieved in this life, whereas the Master postpones this until the hereafter; see Kardong, *Benedict's Rule*, p. 24. For another example of this difference, compare what follows *RM* 10.91 (the end of the Master's chapter on humility) with the end of *RB* 7; the Master gives a flowery description of heaven, which implies that the benefits of humility come in the after-life, whereas Benedict drops this passage and leaves the question open. A. Böckmann, *A Listening Community: A Commentary on the Prologue and Chapters 1–3 of Benedict's Rule* (Collegeville: Liturgical Press, 2015), p. 49, thinks that Benedict's text contains 'a mystical element', as does M. Casey, *The Road to Eternal Life: Reflections on the Prologue of Benedict's Rule* (Collegeville: Liturgical Press, 2011), pp. 85–8.

28 Böckmann, *Perspectives*, p. 79. Unfortunately the significance of the title to *RB* 73 is easily lost in translation because of changes in the meaning of justice (*iustitia*); see *RB 1980*, p. 295, and Kardong, *Benedict's Rule*, pp. 603, 615. Benedict is alluding to Mt 3:15 and 6:33 (which he quotes in *RB* 2.35) At this point Benedict gathers together ideas from Basil, Cassian and Leo the Great.

29 Böckmann, *Perspectives*, p. 82.

Index

abbot 113–17, 119–21, 123, 125–6, 141, 144
Acacius 62, 76
Affile 55–8, 71
Agapitus, Pope 29, 184
Alatri 146
Alexandria 29, 170
Amalasuntha 10, 30, 174, 187, 199–200
Ambrose 51–2, 138, 161, 181–2
Anastasius, Pope 62, 66
Antioch 18, 59
Aquinum 89, 100, 127, 141, 197
Arians/Arianism 21–5, 204–5
 relationship with Catholics 23–4, 26–8, 30–1
aristocracy: see elites
Athalaric 10, 174, 187
Augustine 42, 44–5, 52–3, 90–2, 117, 161, 194–5, 213 n.11

Basil 51, 66, 91
baths 34, 36, 183
Belisarius 10–16, 161–2, 193
Benedict 1–3, 9–10, 16–17, 43–4, 61, 71, 80, 93, 141, 143, 157, 185, 192
 as abbot at Subiaco 83–8, 117–19
 as abbot at Monte Cassino 90, 94–8, 100–1, 106, 117–18, 146
 attitude to Arianism 25–6, 31–2
 and Christological controversy 66–7
 and compunction 153–4
 and contemplation 155
 departure from Rome 55–8
 education 33, 36–8, 41–2, 45
 family background 9, 107, 137, 210 n.4, 222 n.30
 as hermit at Subiaco 81–2
 his holiness in action 102–5
 in Laurentian schism 65–6, 71, 75, 216 n.10
 and the Master 90–2, 162, 220 n.12, 227 n.27
 and Scholastica 147–52, 226 n.15
 his vision 40, 163–5
 see also Gregory, Dialogue 2, miracles described in
Benedict option 162–3
Bible 24, 47, 50–1, 117, 169, 185, 214 n.17
Boethius 28, 42–3, 91, 165–6, 185, 187
books 48–50
bread: see under food
boys 52, 121–2, 131

Caesarius 138, 195
Campania 18, 89, 91, 94, 98–100, 102, 188, 207
Casinum 89, 99
Cassian 51, 66–8, 83, 91, 143, 152, 154, 156, 166–7, 194–5
Cassiodorus 14, 37, 53, 167–8, 174, 185, 206–7

229

cellarer 132–4
Christological controversy 41, 59–61, 67–8, 76–9, 215 n.4
Church 26, 35, 59, 64, 66, 69–70, 76, 80, 101, 109, 115, 121, 148, 157–8, 171, 172–3, 180–1
churches 22–3, 31, 74, 87, 138, 184
tituli churches 35, 70–4, 217 n.20
Cicero 37, 39, 45, 52, 163–4
clothing 126–7, 168–9
codex 49, 169, 214 n.17
Colosseum 34, 36
Columella 173–4, 197
communion 140–1
compunction 152–3
Conditaria 63, 69, 196
consilium 119
Constantinople 5, 13, 18, 28–9, 59, 61, 77–8, 80, 187
contemplation 154–7, 164
Councils of the Church 171, 173
  at Nicaea (325) 21, 24
  at Ephesus (431) 51, 60
  at Chalcedon (451) 51, 61, 67, 76–8, 108
  at Orange (529) 195
  at Constantinople (554) 79
curial class 9, 107–8, 210 n.4
Cyril, patriarch of Alexandria 51, 60–1, 67–8, 77–9, 170

deans 117–8
Dionysius Exiguus 43–4, 68, 78, 91, 138, 171
discipline 114, 120–3, 223 n.7
dispensator 95–7, 100–1, 173
dominus 97, 113–4, 172
Desert Fathers 51, 83, 86, 153

education
  liberal 36–7
  religious 37
  of boys 52
elites
  emigration to East 13–14, 16, 34, 148, 188
  as landowners 9, 14, 94–5, 101
  role in local society 9, 107
  as managers of churches 71–2, 74–5
  as patrons in Rome 72
  as senators 106–7
  their villas 94–5
emperors 5–6, 27, 192
  see also Justin, Justinian
equestrians 107
Eugippius 90–2, 146, 213 n.11
Evagrius 167, 225 n.18

Fathers, of the Church 51, 66
Florentius 87–8, 145
florilegia 45, 51, 91–2, 195, 213 n.11
food
  balanced diet 130–1, 170–1
  bread 127–30, 166, 224 n.18
  distribution in Rome 35, 72–3
  meat 130–1, 185–6
  preparation of 127–30
  preservation of 132–3, 174
  olive oil 130, 133–4
  quantities of 127
  wine 127, 130

Gaul 7, 199
Gelasius, Pope 27, 43, 62–3, 66, 74, 171, 196
Goths 5–6, 10–12, 15–16, 202–3
  military tactics 12–13
  religion 21–25, 212 n.14
  settlement in Italy 7, 9

Index

Gregory the Great, Pope 1–2, 87–8, 109, 151–2, 155–6, 164–5, 175, 177–81, 202
Gregory, *Dialogue 2* 1–2, 55–8, 65, 177–80, 215 n.2; miracles described in 57, 85, 94, 103, 105, 134, 175–7, 178–9, 205–6, 219 n.6
gyrovagues: *see under* monks

Henotikon 62–3, 76
Hormisdas, Pope 27, 76–8
hospitality: *see* visitors
household management 115–17
hymns 41–2, 181–2, 224 n.4

insulae (apartment blocks) 35

Jerome 49. 52, 91, 143
Justin 76–8, 182, 187
Justinian 10, 19, 30–1, 78–80, 109, 158, 162, 182–3, 187, 200, 203

Laurentius/Laurentian 62–5, 69, 71, 216 n.9
Laurentian schism 62–6, 68, 143
lectio divina: see reading
Leo, Pope 61
libraries 34, 36, 50, 52, 183–5
Lombards 11, 158
Lucullanum 90–1, 146

Macrobius 39, 42, 164–5
Manichaeism 27, 185
Mary, the Blessed Virgin 41, 60, 68
Mass 106, 139–140, 142, 144, 157, 221 n.26 224 n.6, 225 n.7
Master 84, 143, 156, 162, 173–4

see also Rule of the Master
Martianus Capella 38, 42
Milan 15, 22–3, 42, 161
monastic economy 86–7, 89, 92–3, 98–100, 163, 219 n.6
monks 102, 111, 123–5, 143, 145, 148, 221 n.26
  gyrovagues 145
  number of 101, 117, 186
  recruits 83
  sarabaites 146–7
Monophysites 60–1, 76–8, 200
Monte Cassino 89, 104, 168
  monastery on 1, 11–12, 17, 42, 86, 90–3, 95, 110, 117, 158–9, 189, 204–5, 220 n.9
  local opposition at 105

Naples 10–12, 15, 30, 203
Neo-Chalcedonianism 78–9
Neoplatonism 39, 44
Nestorius 59–60
nuns 147–9
Nursia 1, 9

Odoacer 5–6
Offices 42, 45, 123, 138–9, 142
opus dei: see prayer
oratory 48, 122, 137

paganism 82, 104–5, 178, 204–5
paterfamilias 113–15, 119, 172
Paulinus 41, 52, 110
perfumes 99–100, 188
plague 18, 162, 188–9
Plombariola 150
popes 189–90
  and sexual *mores* 196
  see also names of individual popes
porter 100
prayer 135, 152, 155
  by Benedict 104

231

Saint Benedict in his Community

contemplative 154–7
in churches 138
in households 69, 137–9, 141, 157
in the monastery 138–9
priests 74, 106, 221 n.28
as monks 142–5
priors 117–8
private ownership 125–6
Procopius 191, 200, 202, 212 n.14
Proba 40, 45, 52, 190
Prudentius 41, 52, 182
punishment: *see* discipline
purple 127, 191

rank
in Roman society 106–8, 110–11
in the monastery 123–5, 134–5
Ravenna 5, 10, 14–15, 22, 28–9, 199
reading 45–7, 214 n.13
Rimini 15, 63
Rome 1, 7, 15–16, 22–3, 33–6, 55–8, 62, 98, 138, 175
sieges of 13, 31
plan for the destruction of 192–3
Rule of Benedict 48, 66, 83–4, 90–2, 96, 117, 143, 150, 220 n.10, 220 n.12
Rule of the Master 84, 90–2, 116, 162, 220 n.12, 227 n.27

Sant' Agata dei Goti, church of 22–3
Sant' Apollinare Nuovo, church of 23, 25, 193–4
Santa Maria Maggiore, cathedral of 34
Saint Peter's basilica 63–4, 73, 218 n.22

sarabaites 146–7
Scholastica 147, 149–52, 226 n.15
Sedulius 41–2, 52, 182
semi-Pelagianism 194–6
senate 5, 8, 14, 106–7, 193
senpectae 118, 121, 144
Servandus 145
sheep farming 97, 196–7
Silverius, Pope 29, 201
slaves 95, 108–10, 197–8
Subiaco 1, 81, 219 n.4
monastery at 85–8, 117–18
Symmachus, Pope 62–5, 68–9, 71, 73–4, 171

tablets 46–7, 207–8
Terracina 89–90, 118
Theodahad 14, 29–30, 174, 187
Theoderic 6–10, 14, 62–4, 187, 198–199
political policy of 8–9
religious policy of 26–9, 216 n.9
Theodora 162, 183, 200–1
Theopaschite confession 77–9
Three Chapters controversy 79–80
Tivoli 15, 86, 202
Totila 11–16, 174, 192–3, 202–3
his meeting with Benedict 12, 201–2

Vandals 22, 26, 161, 183, 199
Varro, Marcus Terentius 38, 52
Verona 10, 28
Vesuvius 18, 211 n.17
Vicovaro 1, 83, 147, 219 n.1
Vigilius, Pope 79, 200–1
vilicus 95–7, 173, 197
Virgil 37, 38–9, 40–2, 45, 53

232

Index

Visigoths   22, 199
visitors to the monastery   17, 203–5

war in Italy   10–19, 30, 211 n.1
water supply   85–6, 205–6

weather   18, 98–9, 206–7, 211 n.17
work   93–4, 97–9, 127–9, 135–6, 173–4
wine: *see under* food
workshop   89, 99